THE

HBCU

EXPERIENCE

THE TENNESSEE STATE UNIVERSITY EDITION

Visionary Author Ashley Little
Lead Author Ashlee Brooks
Foreword Author Dr Tameka Winston
Foreword Author Brenda Gilmore

For permission requests, write to the publisher, addressed|

"Attention Permissions Coordinator," at
thehbcuexperiencemovement@gmail.com

Book Cover Design: The Harbor Institute

Published By: The HBCU Experience Movement, LLC

The HBCU Experience Movement, LLC

thehbcuexperiencemovement@gmail.com
www.thehbcuexperiencemovement.com

Ordering Information:

Quantity Sales: Special discounts are available on quantity purchases by corporations, associations, and nonprofits. For details, contact the publisher at the address above.

ISBN: 978-1-7349311-0-5

A Message from the Founders
Ashley Little, Fred Whit & Uche Byrd

Historically Black Colleges & Universities (HBCUs) were established to serve the educational needs of black Americans. During the time of their establishment, and many years afterward, blacks were generally denied admission to traditionally white institutions. Prior to The Civil War, there was no structured higher education system for black students. Public policy, and certain statutory provisions, prohibited the education of blacks in various parts of the nation. Today, HBCUs represent a vital component of American higher education.

The HBCU Experience Movement, LLC is a collection of stories from prominent alumni throughout the world, who share how their HBCU experience molded them into the people they are today. We are also investing financially into HBCUs throughout the country. Our goal is to create a global movement of prominent HBCU alumni throughout the nation to continue to share their stories each year, allowing us to give back to prestigious HBCUs annually.

We are proud to present to you *The HBCU Experience: The Tennessee State University Edition.* We would like to acknowledge and give a special thanks to our amazing lead author, Ashlee Brooks, for your dedication and commitment. We appreciate you and thank you for your hard work and dedication on behalf of this project. We would also like to give a special thanks to our headliner, foreword authors, contributing authors and partners of Tennessee State University for believing in this movement and investing your time, and monetary donations, to give back to your school. We appreciate all of the Tennessee State University alumni who shared your HBCU experience in this publication.

i

ASHLEY LITTLE

About Ashley Little

Ashley Little is The CEO/Founder of Ashley Little Enterprises, LLC which encompasses her Media, Consulting Work, Writing, Ghost Writing, Book Publishing, Book Coaching, Project Management, Public Relations & Marketing, and Empowerment Speaking. In addition, she is an Award-Winning Serial Entrepreneur, TV/Radio Host, Speaker, Host, Philanthropist, Investor and 5X Best Selling Author.

She is a proud member of Delta Sigma Theta Sorority Incorporated, and a member of Alpha Phi Omega. She is very involved in her community, organizations and non-profits. Currently, she is the Co-Founder of Sweetheart Scholars Non-profit Organization 501 (C-3) along with three other powerful women. This scholarship is given out annually to African American Females from her hometown of Wadesboro, North Carolina who are attending college to help with their expenses. Ms. Little believes it takes a village to raise a child and to never forget where you come from. Ms. Little is a strong believer in giving back to her community. She believes our young ladies need vision, direction, and strong mentorship. She is the Head of the Scholarship Committee for Swing Into Their Dreams Foundation the mission of Swing Into Their Dream Foundation is E.P.I.C. Empowerment and Philanthropy In The Community.

She is the Founder and Owner of T.A.L.K Radio & TV Network, LLC. Airs in over 167 countries, streamed LIVE on Facebook, YouTube, Twitter and Periscope. Broadcasting and Media Production Company. This live entertainment platform is for new or existing radio shows, television shows, or other electronic media outlets, to air content from a centralized source. All news, information or music shared on this platform are solely the responsibility of the station/radio owner. She is also the Owner and Creator of Creative Broadcasting Radio Station the station of "unlimited possibilities" and Podcast, Radio/TV Host. She is also one of the hosts of the new TV Show Daytime Drama National Syndicated Television Show which will be aired on Comcast Channel 19 and ATT Channel 99 in 19 Middle Tennessee Counties. It will also air on The United Broadcasting

Network, The Damascus Roads Broadcasting Network, and Roku. She is CEO/Co-Founder of The HBCU Experience Movement LLC and CEO/Founder of Little Publishing LLC.

Ms. Little is a 5X Best Selling Author of "Dear Fear, Volume 2 18 Powerful Lessons Of Living Your Best Life Outside Of Fear", "The Gyrlfriend Code Volume 1", "I Survived", "Girl Get Up, and Win", "Glambitious Guide to Being An Entrepreneur", The Making Of A Successful Business Woman, and "Hello Queen". She is a Co-Host for The Tamie Collins Markee Radio Show, Award-Winning Entrepreneur, Reflection Contributor for the book "NC Girls Living In A Maryland World, Sales/Marketing/Contributing Writer/Event Correspondent for SwagHer Magazine, Contributing Writer for MizCEO Magazine, Contributing Editor for SheIs Magazine, ContributingWriter/National Sales Executive for Courageous Woman Magazine, Contributing Writer for Upwords International Magazine (India), Contributing Writer/Global Partner for Powerhouse Global International Magazine(London), Host of "Creating Your Seat At The Table", Host of "Authors On The Rise", Co-Host Glambitious Podcast, Partner/Visionary Author of The Gyrlfriend Code The Sorority Edition along with The Gyrlfriend Collective, LLC and Lead Author of The HBCU Experience The North Carolina A&T State University Edition. She has been on many different Podcasts, TV Shows, Magazines, and Radio Shows. Lastly, she has received awards such as "Author Of The Month", The Executive Citation of Anne Arundel County, Maryland Award which was awarded by the County Executive Steuart L. Pittman, Top 28 Influential Business Pioneers for K.I.S.H Magazine Spring 2019 Edition. She has been featured in SwagHer Magazine, Power20Magazine Glambitious, Sheen Magazine, All About Inspire Magazine, Formidable Magazine, BRAG Magazine, Sheen Magazine, Front Cover of MizCEO Magazine November 2019, Front Cover for UpWords Magazine October 2019 Edition, Courageous Woman Magazine, Courageous Woman Special Speakers Edition November 2019, Influence Magazine, Featured/Interviewed On a National Syndicated Television Show HBCU 101 on Aspire TV, Dynasty of Dreamers K.I.S.H Magazine Spring 2019 Edition, Dynasty of Dreamers K.I.S.H Magazine September 2019 Edition, Front Cover of Courageous Magazine December 2019, Front

Cover of Doz International Magazine January 2020, Top 28 Influential Business Pioneers for K.I.S.H Magazine, Power20 Magazine Glambitious January 2020, Power20 Magazine Glambitious February 2020, Featured in Powerhouse Global International London Magazine March 2020 edition, Featured in Sheen Magazine February 2020 as one of "The Top 20 Women To Be On The Lookout For In 2020, Awarded National Women's Empowerment Ministry "Young, Gifted, & Black Award" February 2020 which honors and celebrate women in business such as Senior Level Executives, Entrepreneurs and CEO's below age 40 for their creativity and business development. Featured in National Women Empowerment Magazine 2020 as well to name a few.

Ms. Little received her undergraduate degree in English from North Carolina A&T State University. Next, she received her Master's Degree in Industrial Organizational Psychology. Ms. Little is a mover and shaker and she continuously pushes herself to be better than she was yesterday. She gives GOD all the credit for everything that has happened in her life. She has strong faith and determination to be great. She believes her only competition is herself. Her favorite scripture is Philippians 4:13 "I can do all things through Christ who strengthens me".

UCHE BYRD

About Uche Byrd

Uche Byrd was born and raised on the Southside of Chicago. As a graduate from The North Carolina Agricultural and Technical State University, Uche not only obtained his Bachelor's degree in Applied Mathematics, but he also went on to earn a Master's degree in Industrial Engineering. During his tenure at the HBCU, Uche was fortunate enough to pledge the Mu Psi Chapter of Omega Psi Phi Fraternity, Inc., as well as to hold the position of Mr. Aggie. Uche also served as the Region 2 Pre-College Initiative Chair for the National Society of Black Engineers and Vice President of the Midwest Aggie Club. As a Resident Assistant at The Aggie Suites, Uche was a mentor and motivation to many. Today, Uche resides in northeast Washington, D.C. with his wife and son, and serves as the Metro Area Youth Federation Leader for the Allegheny East Conference of the Seventh-Day Adventist Church, where he works with the youth programing for 30+ churches in the D.C., Maryland and Virginia areas.

FRED WHITAKER

About Fred Whitaker

When passion, performance and perseverance come together, a force to be reckoned with is created. Frederick Whitaker, known industry-wide as Fred Whit, has become a well-known name due to his business strategies and negotiative saavy, behind the scenes of the entertainment industry. He is a believer in the mantra hard work pays off, and has lived this mantra everyday of his professional life.

These days, stars such as actor and media personalities Terrence J and La La Anthony, filmmaker Will Packer, and a host of others, call on him when they need unique jobs done in a professional and dignified manner. He rises to any occasion and consistently exceeds expectations.

Growing up between the make or break city of New York and resolute small towns of rural North Carolina, Fred developed his acumen as a polished businessman. New York introduced Fred to the meaning of "hustle" and "ambition" with North Carolina yielding a certain Southern compassion and charm. Now the man the industry sees has the experience and ability to single-handedly take numerous careers to the next level.

As manager of Terrence J (*E! News, Think Like A Man1 & 2*) he secures major roles and television deals and brand integration for the rising star. Fred was instrumental in Terrence landing exclusive endorsements with Crown Royal and Jeep. In addition, Fred successfully planned the rollout for La La Anthony's *New York Times* best seller book, *The Love Playbook: Rules for Love, Sex, and Happiness*. Furthermore, Fred consults for radio host Angela Yee NYC's Power 105 morning show) with more deals in the works. Wearing many hats, he never loses sight of his main goal – to provide incomparable service for each of his clients. Fred proves, as his company motto states, it is the little things you do in life that make all the difference.

Fred has always had a knack for making something out of nothing. While in college at NC A&T State University, he coordinated various large campus events. After graduating with a degree in communications, Fred took steps on a path he didn't imagine himself traveling. "I had no experience in management, so everything I have accomplished over the last fifteen years, I learned on the job," he states. One many occasions he's played the role of assistant, manager, accountant, provided service to whatever was needed for completion. As is this isn't enough, Fred has also negotiated several deals with McDonald's, Sean John, and Samsung, as he goes on to gain favor across multiple branding platforms.

A devout humanitarian, he makes time to organize charity events, toy drives, raising funds and giving away almost $10,000 worth of clothes to the Salvation Army, annually. Fred finds it difficult to build his empire without breathing life into the progress of others.

Success is measured by loving what you do, and making things happen while doing it. As doors continue to open, Fred will never forget those moments where his destiny was uncertain, but he believed his dreams of success would certainly come true. Those dreams have not only come into fruition, they are growing far beyond his imagination. An admirable being and determined man, Fred Whitaker has become a staple in the industry, all while shaping the lives of not only those who achieve fame, but everyday people as well.

TABLE OF CONTENTS

DR. TAMEKA WINSTON

Foreword

After reading about the unique experiences of Tennessee State University Alumni who are blazing trails in their perspective fields, readers will walk away feeling inspired and affirmed. TSU has produced some of the best and brightest across the globe. The endearing reflections will also provide a deeper understanding of why Historically Black Colleges and Universities are an intricate part of our respective histories.

When in need of motivation, I play "Lift Every Voice and Sing" and there is an immediate connection with the ancestors after the first few lines. This book will serve as motivation to current and future TSU Tigers just as I am inspired by the beautiful hymn written by my favorite scholar, James Weldon Johnson and his brother John Johnson. Many of those before us turned to HBCUs to find refuge and solid ground during some of the most horrific times for African Americans.

Although my late maternal grandmother did not have the opportunity to attend college, she instilled in me a desire to live out her wildest dreams. It is a privilege to serve as a Professor and Associate Vice President of Research and Sponsored Programs at the university nestled by the shores of the Cumberland. As a proud faculty member, I've had the unique opportunity to work with some of the most talented students across the country and internationally. They are ambitious and ready to make their mark on the world.

One of my fondest memories as a child was going to the library. Because I grew up in a very small town in rural Mississippi, books helped me understand at a very young age that there was a way of living outside of the life that I saw each day. I am certain that this book will have the same impact on future HBCU students who will pick up this impassioned, personal yet sophisticated piece and immediately discover that the possibilities are endless. I am a proud HBCU graduate and I know without a doubt there is nothing quite like the HBCU experience. This book has been designed to be used by HBCU supporters and academic audiences. In short, this is the book about TSU Tiger Alumni that we have been waiting for.

Dr. Tameka T. Winston

Associate Vice President of Research and Sponsored Programs

Chair, Department of Communications

Tennessee State University

Foreword Author Dr. Tameka Winston

Dr. Tameka Winston is the Associate Vice President of Research and Sponsored Programs, Department Chair and an award-winning Professor in the Department of Communications at Tennessee State University. She is also a national radio show host on Sirius XM and an accomplished author. Winston has been working at the collegiate level for 17 years in various roles. Because of her stellar research agenda, Dr. Winston was awarded tenure. She was recently described by former Nashville Mayor Megan Barry as a true powerhouse in the field of higher education.

This longtime educator is the founder of 3 mentoring programs geared towards assisting individuals in the Nashville community and beyond. Powerful testimonials from Winston's mentees reveal that she is dedicated to helping others reach their fullest potential. Her passion for education and community service has helped her earn several accolades. A highly sought-after speaker, she also facilitates numerous workshops on various topics. She is among this year's Class of 2018 protégés for the American Association of State Colleges and Universities' (AASCU) Millennium Leadership Initiative Institute in Washington, DC. The purpose of the highly selective Millennium Leadership Initiative (MLI) is to prepare, enhance and advance the prospect for qualified candidates, who have progressed in their professional careers, to successfully compete in the future for positions of president or chancellor at universities or colleges, public or private.

Dr. Winston was recently awarded the "2018 Leading Young Alumni Award" from her alma mater (Alcorn State University). She was also awarded the prestigious 2017 Athena Young Professional Leadership Award. Winston received the Nashville Business Journal's "2017 Woman of Influence Award". She received the 2015 Woman of Achievement Award at the 35th Annual Women in Higher Education in Tennessee conference. Past award recipients include Dr. Shirley Raines who is the first female president of the University of Memphis. The Woman of Achievement Award is presented to a dedicated leader who has earned admiration and respect, has vision and leads by example, faces challenges with grace and courage, and lives with dignity, integrity and honor. For three years in a row, Winston has been named a Nashville Emerging Leader finalist in the category of Education. Because of her accomplishments in the field of Education, TSU President Glenda Glover awarded Dr. Winston with the 2018 Woman of Legend and Merit Award. She also received the 2018 Black Nashville Honors Award alongside renowned gospel artist Bobby Jones and 4 other African Americans who are dedicated to making a difference in the community.

Nashville Lifestyle Magazine named Winston one of Nashville's 25 Most Beautiful People. Winston was awarded the 2015-2016 Professor of Year Award by the College of Liberal Arts. She was also awarded the 2012-2013 Professor of the Year Award. Not only was she chosen as one of the Nashville Business Journal's Top 40 Under 40 but she was also selected as one of the Network Journal's 2015 "40 Under Forty" Dynamic Achievers in the United States. The national award recognizes outstanding young African-Americans who are "Reaching for Higher Goals" in their careers while remaining dedicated to their community's development. Notable past honorees include renowned journalist Soledad O'Brien.

Winston is also a Young Leaders Council alumna. She is very passionate about promoting the importance of having strong mentorship programs in place. One of her mentoring programs (Black Docs Mentoring) specializes in mentoring scholars of color throughout the United States who are interested in pursuing their doctoral degree. Several of her mentees have received their doctoral degree from various universities throughout the country.

Her latest mentorship program is geared towards students from various universities in the Nashville area affected by the death of a parent/primary caregiver. Two students will be selected and added to the program each academic year. She will connect each mentee with a licensed psychologist. Winston is an advocate for mental health and she spends a significant amount of time helping to eliminate the stigma and improve access/treatment in the local community and nationwide. The mentees receive care packages each semester that will consist of items that are useful to college students. The care package will also include contact information for an assigned licensed psychologist if needed, snacks, school supplies and other things deemed appropriate. Dr. Winston will work closely with the students/mentees throughout their time in college.

Recently, she worked closely with the Tennessean to organize the department's first endowed scholarship (Getahn Ward Memorial Scholarship). The scholarship was created in honor of the late TSU professor and longtime Tennessean business reporter, Mr. Getahn Ward. Because of Mr. Ward's dedication to the community, the department and the field of journalism, Winston's vision was to acknowledge him in a permanent way by naming the department's newsroom in his honor.

Winston researched and developed the entire print curriculum for the department, which incorporates new media technologies and multimedia convergence. Also, she is the first in the department to develop and teach a course that is offered solely online. Her research interests include coverage of education related issues in the media, media convergence, new media technologies, multimedia curriculum and the status of education in the black belt states.

Dr. Winston has been featured in various print and broadcast media outlets including Fox 17/ WZTV, WKRN, The Tennessee Tribune, Nashville Business Journal, Nashville Lifestyle Magazine, the Network Journal, The Tennessean and many more. She has also authored several books. These include "Understanding the Speechmaking Process", "Introducing the Speechmaking Process" and "Mass Media Revolution". "Understanding the Speechmaking Process" is currently being used at the university for the Public Speaking course. "Mass Media Revolution" is one of the top selling Mass Communications textbooks in the country. A fourth book (Mastering the Speechmaking Process) is scheduled to be released later this year.

Dr. Winston's voice can be heard each week anywhere in the United States because of her national radio show that she refers to as a great platform to inspire others to reach their fullest potential. She also created both shows. The two shows are Black Docs and Tennessee State Talks. Winston currently serves a mentor for the Music City Girls Lead Program. She also served as a mentor for the annual Nashville Business Journal's Mentor Monday for the past 4 years. She is a member of several civic organizations including Links, Incorporated and Alpha Kappa Alpha Sorority, Incorporated. She is also a member of the Rotary Club of Nashville.

Not only does Dr. Winston work hard to serve the Nashville community, she has several international service projects. Dr. Winston is the creator and project director of the AGBOR/Nigeria initiative. She is working closely with administrators from 2 universities in Nigeria to launch two academic programs. She is also the founder of the AGBOR Nigeria book project. Winston collects and sends books to the AGBOR community in Nigeria. She is extremely passionate about her international service. Winston is also passionate about assisting Nigeria by providing resources (books and other educational materials) to benefit students in the K-12 setting.

Winston earned her Doctoral Degree and Specialist in Education Degree at Tennessee State University, has a Master's Degree from Austin Peay State University, and a B.A. from Alcorn State University. She enjoys writing and spending time with her husband.

SENATOR BRENDA GILMORE

Foreword

My journey to Tennessee State University (TSU) began in Gallatin, Tennessee. I was raised in a small, close-knit community of God-loving people who taught me to hope, dream, and to believe that all things were possible. Growing up, I encountered TSU alumni from time to time, and I was mesmerized by the manner that they carried themselves and how they were leaders in the community. As a young girl, I decided that I too wanted to be a part of this community. I wanted to achieve big things and touch the lives of others for the betterment of my community.

I was able to achieve my dream and enroll in the Tennessee State University and to become a Tiger! From the very beginning, my TSU experience was more than I could have ever hoped and has enriched my life experiences in ways that I cherish to this very day.

First, I had never seen so many African-American educators and professionals in my life. In them, I saw myself and began to truly conceptualize that I could be a proud, strong black woman who was educated, respected, and a leader. The HBCU experience is so important for people like me who were not exposed, to a great extent, to such highly educated and professionally accomplished African-Americans. Sometimes, the truth is that you must first see someone who looks like you in a position before you truly know that you can do it to.

The second experience that was amazing and that I still cherish and enjoy to this day is the camaraderie and togetherness that I experienced at TSU. Most of my classmates carried a great sense of pride and fellowship in being a TSU Tiger. We knew of the rich history and tradition of our school and wanted to add on to this legacy in our on little way. We encouraged each other, helped each other, prayed with each other, and loved each other. TSU was more than a university. It was a family and home away from home. Ever since I joined the TSU family, I have always had true friends and colleagues backing me up and caring for me. I have talked to many people about their college experience, and their experiences just do not equal the TSU and HBCU experience. The brother and sisterhood of our institutions are unraveled anywhere.

A third aspect of my TSU experience that continues to pay huge dividends for me was the excellent learning environment and superior professors that taught me. Unlike many other universities, TSU's professors cared and were devoted to their students. I had so many professors take their time in and out of the classroom to encourage me and others that we could achieve anything that we dreamed. Their extraordinary knowledge of their subject matter areas also provided me a foundation to face any intellectual and professional challenge that I have encountered. I was exposed to a rigorous and rewarding academic environment where greatness was the standard.

Because of the high academic standards of learning and the historic expectations that we carry, TSU, along with other HBCUs, produce a disproportionally high percentage of America's black business executives, political leaders, attorneys, doctors, educators, spiritual leaders, and community activists. As a Nashville elected official, I know firsthand that TSU alumni are significantly responsible for the growth in Nashville and for the leadership of our black community. Without TSU and other HBCUs, America and the black community would be deprived of millions of leaders who truly make our country great.

After graduating from TSU, I have been blessed with continued fellowship and connections. Joining an HBCU is like joining a supportive and loving family. Since I graduated, I still enjoy going to TSU alumni functions, and attending TSU sporting events and showing my Tiger pride! And, a TSU Homecoming is like no other experience. It may be imitated by many other universities, but it is never duplicated!

In my professional career, I cannot put into words how important and valuable TSU has been to me. At TSU, I developed a deeper and greater appreciation for service, particularly helping students.

During my time in higher education, I mentored students, gave hundreds of people job opportunities, and mentored my employees to advance in their own careers. I was able to have the type of career that I had envisioned for myself. TSU helped give me the confidence, determination, intellectual firepower, and appreciation for service to others.

My next journey has been as a public servant and official in my beloved city of Nashville. I never dreamed that I would run for public office. But, I had always believed in serving and uplifting others. Even as a teenager, I taught Sunday school. Now, I must confess that I am not sure why I was entrusted to teach Sunday school being so young, but praise God anyway. In this role, I would organize my Sunday school class to put together care packages for senior citizens. I encouraged others to make people's lives better. So, although service was deep in my bones from an early stage, TSU fortified my belief in service.

Even though it took a while to sprout, TSU planted a seed that grew inside of me to serve my community in greater roles.

Much later in life, I was asked to work on a local candidate's campaign, and I agreed. During the campaign, my neighbors started noticing that people were willing to help when I asked them to do something. People began to tell me that I was a good community leader. I just thought I was being passionate and dedicated. Eventually, I decided that I would run for the city council. It was a risky and big decision in my life. But, I reflected on my time at TSU and the inspiration and example that my professors and administrators had on me. I knew that I was prepared and ready. I knew that I could meet the challenge, because I was a TSU Tiger! After a tough race, I won the election.

Subsequently, by the grace of God and the great people of my community, I was elected to serve in the Tennessee House of Representatives. I was blessed to serve in this role for 12 years. Then, in November 2018, I was blessed to be elected State Senator for the 19th District of the Tennessee Senate. There is no way that I could have achieved these positions of leadership without my experience and connection with TSU. TSU instilled the confidence, determination, and knowledge in me to light my torch for the world to see.

Today, I fight for better schools, public school teachers, criminal justice reform, a higher minimum wage, gender equity, economic empowerment for poor and working people, and for children. There are still significant battles for progress and equality that must be won. But, TSU and HBCUs have a tremendous history of producing brilliant minds to continue to fight these battles. These struggles are not always won over night or even in a lifetime. This is why HBCUs are so important and critical to the progress of African-Americans and working people in America.

I could not be any happier about my college experience and what it has allowed me to do. I have had a life and career that can only be described as truly blessed and fortunate. Without a shadow of a doubt, TSU played an indispensable part in my success. From providing inspiration, excellent learning and mentorships, lifelong friends, and a supportive family environment, TSU has been an amazing asset and rewarding resource in my life through the years.

We all must continue to support our HBCUs, so that they will remain a powerful presence in our community. Without HBCUs, our communities will have little to no hope of meeting the difficult challenges that we face. If we all donate and support our HBCUs, we can ensure that future generations of Americans will have the opportunity to find knowledge, pride, and family in great institutions of higher learning.

Additionally, I would encourage every young person to strongly consider attending a HBCU. If you commit yourself to a cause greater than yourself, you will have a rewarding career and life as well. Go Big Blue!

Sincerely Yours,

Brenda Gilmore

Foreword Author Senator Brenda Gilmore

Brenda Gilmore was elected State Senator, District #19 for the State of Tennessee, November 2018. She is a former Metro Council Woman and served as State Representative, District #54, in the Tennessee General Assembly for twelve years.

Prior employment included almost twenty years as Director of University Mail Services for Vanderbilt. Employment has also included Loan Officer of Fidelity Federal Savings & Loan Association and Director, Postal Services Division, State of Tennessee.

Senator Gilmore holds a Bachelor of Science, Business Degree from Tennessee State University and earned a Master Degree from Vanderbilt University.

Brenda has also formerly served on the Board of the John F. Kennedy Susan Gray School for Children who have been abused and with special needs; Chairperson, Board of Margaret Cunningham Women's Center; Advisor, and Undergraduate Chapter of Delta Sigma Theta Sorority.

Other community involvements have included Chairperson for the United Negro College Fund Volunteer Committee. She has served as the President of the Senior Citizen Inc. Board; the Board of Directors of Skyline Medical Center and Trustee for the Belmont Board of Trust.

Mrs. Gilmore works in the Tennessee State University Alumni Association. She is a member of WIN, Nashville Women Political Caucus, and Chair of the Nominating Committee, League of Women Voters. Brenda is the former President of CABLE, a women's business organization of over 500 women.

She is a Lifetime Member of the NAACP, and holds membership in the Music City Chapter of Links, Chair, Arts Committee, Top Ladies of Distinction and the former President of the National Hook Up of Black Women, and the Minerva Foundation of Delta Sigma Theta Inc.

Brenda Co-Chaired the capital campaign for the Northwest YMCA and successfully raised almost $4 million dollars for an indoor swimming pool. She previously served on the board of Middle Tennessee YMCA, and has chaired the We Build People for the YMCA, raising over $100 thousand dollars for scholarships.

In the Tennessee General Assembly, House of Representatives, she was on the Fiscal Review Committee, the Budget and Finance Committee and the Business and Utility. Rep. Gilmore is the former chair of the Tennessee Black Caucus of the State Legislators, and Co-Chair of the STEM Caucus.

Nationally, she is a board member of the National Caucus of Environmental Legislators, former Director of Women in Government and chair of the Women's Network, National Council of State Legislators, and a member of the Executive Board of the National Black Caucus of State Legislators.

Most recently, Rep. Gilmore Chaired the Women's March 2018, which drew over 15,000 women and men to Nashville to advocate for women's equality.

In Delta, she has chaired numerous chapter committees, served as the President of the Minerva Foundation, State Coordinator of Social Action, and member of the Regional Leadership Team and is presently on the Social Action Commission.

Brenda has received numerous awards. She and her husband, Harry has been married for 46 years. They have one daughter, Councilwoman at Large Erica Gilmore and one granddaughter, Anyah Gilmore Jones, who is a college freshman.

Mrs. Gilmore is a member of Mt. Zion Baptist Church. She works with passion for issues affecting poor people, disadvantaged, women and children.

ASHLEE BROOKS

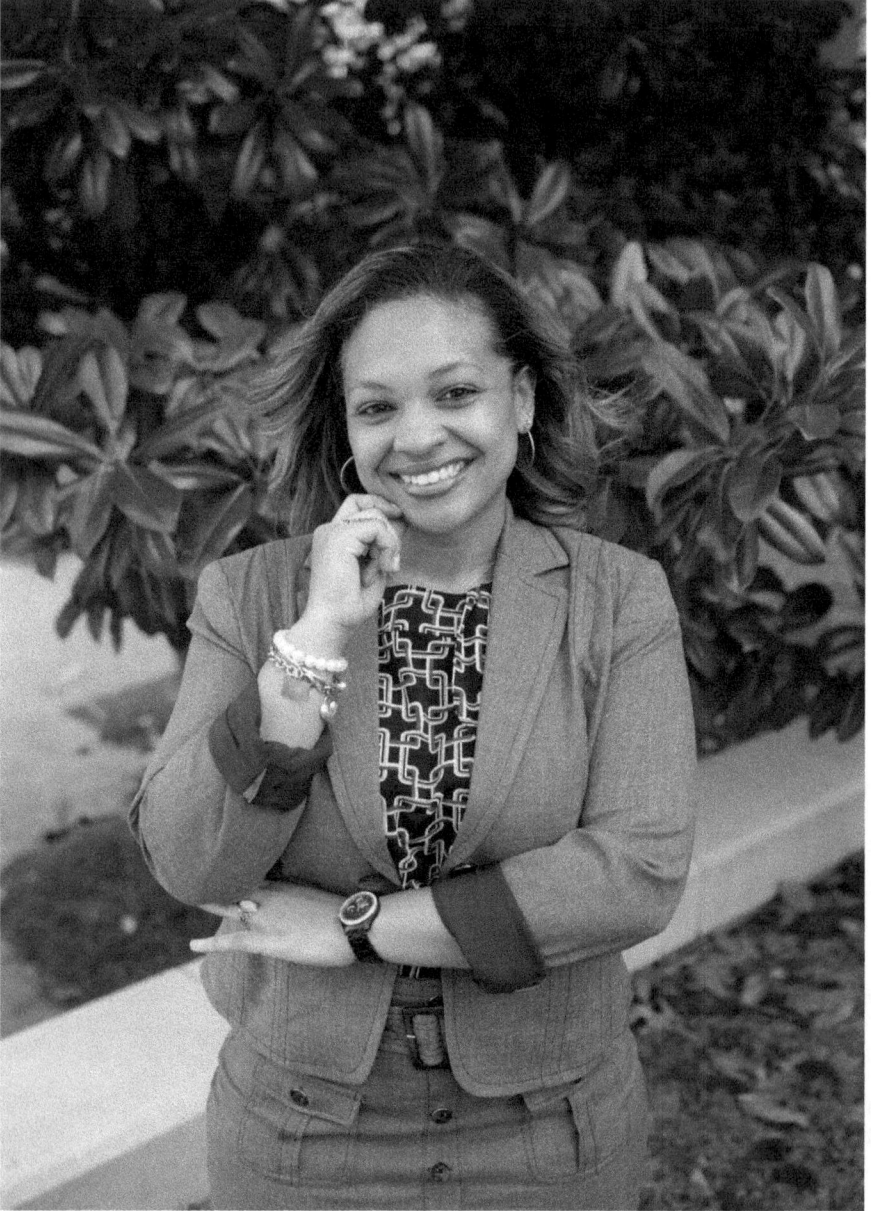

Introduction

When I think of Tennessee State University, the first person who comes to mind is Morris T. Goodard. Class of 1962, my adored godfather, affectionately known as "G."

When deciding where I wanted to attend college, my sights were set on Atlanta, Georgia.

I wanted to move out of Memphis. I wanted to move out of Tennessee and explore the unknown. Throughout my senior year of high school, G continued to encourage me to attend Tennessee State University. He provided me with numerous pamphlets, newspaper clippings and applications to broaden my knowledge of what Historically Black Colleges and Universities (HBCUs) had to offer. My parents encouraged me to stay home and attend the prestigious Rhodes College. However, I must admit, before G, I wasn't privy to why attending a HBCU held such high esteem.

As fate would have it, in August of 2002, I was headed to Nashville, Tennessee to begin my life in the "Land of Golden Sunshine." Little did I know this would be one of the most rewarding decisions I'd ever make, which continues to impact my life today. I left Memphis, Tennessee, missing my family and friends. I didn't realize that, throughout my enrollment at TSU, I would gain an extended family that would grow by leaps and bounds throughout the years and even surpass my four years at State. My relationships with TSU alums run deep from the 1960s to present day. I continually meet new TSU alums regularly, and I embrace every one of them into our ever-growing family.

Family… family is important to me. My TSU Family… I would ride with my TSU family until the wheels fall off. Most of my memorable experiences were with my TSU family—from living in "The Zoo" (the girls' freshmen dormitory), going to The Sub, walking to Wendy's, to attending my first homecoming game and landing my first internship. In addition,

I became a proud member of Alpha Kappa Alpha Sorority, Incorporated and Phi Beta Lambda Business Fraternity, Inc. I was exposed to so many different things and people that would have an unforgettable impact on my life.

When I graduated from TSU, I set my sights on Tucson, Arizona. There, I was compelled to initiate a Tennessee State University National Alumni Association (TSUNAA) Virtual Alumni Chapter. I wanted to attend every college fair I could to make others aware of my beloved alma mater. In addition, I wanted to highlight what HBCUs had to offer.

Through these initiatives, I fostered many relationships with alumni who graduated before me and even after me. With each move to Richmond, Virginia, to Dallas, Texas and even relocating back to Nashville, I was always able to connect with TSU alum. In Richmond, one of my classmates connected me with his sister, who became one of my lifelong friends. In Dallas,

I was introduced to so many TSU alums that we built our own little community during my four years there. Moving back to Nashville, I was able to reconnect with my TSU classmates and, over the years, we continue to reminisce on our time on the "Yard" as we start our own families and foster a deeper relationship.

Coming from a single-parent household, I didn't have family in the cities that I moved to over the years. Despite the unknown, my TSU family welcomed me with open arms and didn't hesitate to make me feel comfortable. They were always willing to help me and take me in as one of their own. This outpouring of love and support truly inspired me to continue to foster relationships and build bridges between those before and after me. I appreciated the significance of those relationships. It was an indescribable bond that would continue to have everlasting impact on my journey.

When I think of what Tennessee State University means to me, endurance, perseverance, determination, exploration and sense of self are just a few words that come to mind. Upon entering the doors of our Big Blue Country, it was echoed in the Amphitheater, "Look to your left. Look to your right. In the next four years, the person sitting next to you will not be at the end of the finish line with you." At the time, I didn't understand the significance of this message. But as time went on, it became crystal clear. We all may start on the same path. But through trial, tribulations and discovery, it's not guaranteed that we will all end up at the finish line. Some took different journeys, while others pursued endeavors outside of education. Others simply moved back to their hometown. Those who stood on the other side of the Cumberland River with me weathered the storm.

We were able to see the "fertile shores" and continue to flourish beyond our potential ignited at Tennessee State University. As alums, we received our education at TSU. But we also gained insight. We identified our purpose, and we were pushed to strive for more than the status quo. TSU gave me a sense of pride. But, more than anything, it gave me a sense of self and identity. The Ashlee Brooks I am today would not be as passionate and driven if I would have pursued my education someplace else. TSU molded me to continue fostering relationships and to give back.

The HBCU experience gives alums an undeniable sense of pride. We all have similarities; however, when being surrounded by those from various walks of life, it is motivating that we can do *anything* as long as we continue to *Think, Work* and *Serve*. No matter the amount of time that has gone by, we always pick up where we left off. We continue to strengthen our bonds and foster new relationships. Our bonds extend beyond the Land of Golden Sunshine.

As each story is told, the common message that will continue to ring true is that you will never meet a stranger coming from Tennessee State University. The TSU pride and comradery are infectious. Our blue blood runs through and through. In listening to the countless TSU stories from past generations, it bridges the gap with our youth and community. Our TSU spirit is always on display, no matter where we go or what city we live in. The band, homecoming, pep rallies, Greek Week, The Courtyard and The Student Center are all staples in TSU's history. When I entered Tennessee State University, I heard time and time again that it was known as a party school more than known for its academics. In reading these authors' stories, you will realize that TSU is known for molding great leaders, entrepreneurs and trailblazers.

In writing this book, I wanted our alumni to share their TSU experiences and how those experiences impacted their life's journey. We all grew up differently and we all come from various walks of life, with many obstacles along the way. Yet, Tennessee State University brought us together. Through the years, we have forged an unbreakable bond that helped us overcome and encourage one another. My hope is that, through each story shared, you'll learn more about how the legacy of an HBCU—our HBCU—is stitched into the cloth of our lineage.

I didn't understand why it was important to attend a Historically Black College until I walked out of the doors of TSU.

I thought every school was the same. It's something about HBCUs that gives you a little more confidence. It encourages you to create a table if you cannot find a table to sit at. The person who entered Tennessee State University is not the same person who went on to strive for excellence. It's not the same person who learned not to settle for mediocrity or complacency.

Like the other phenomenal authors highlighted in this book, TSU instilled a passion and purpose in me like no other college or university could. TSU ignited a desire in me so deep to go and make a mark on this world. I am always amazed, impressed and inspired by every TSU alum I meet, especially when I learn their story. When selecting each author to be a part of this collaboration, I was confident that we would continue to excel beyond our wildest dreams and embark upon the legacy set by our ancestors. We will continue to break the negative stigma of how Historically Black Colleges and Universities are perceived. Most of us are first-generation trendsetters across many industries. Some were even courageous enough to create their own lane to stand out. We are generational wealth builders. This, by and large, is due to the contributions of Tennessee State University. And this books series is just the first edition of many more to come.

I will always be a proud alum of the Tennessee State University because I "Think. Work. Serve." This motto is a common thread that binds and motivates us to continue to strive for excellence. Tennessee State University is an institution I will always adore. I am forever indebted to my alma mater as I continue to be of service.

We love our white and blue!

Lead Author Ashlee Brooks

About Ashlee Brooks

Ashlee Brooks, is a native of Memphis, TN and a proud alumni of Tennessee State University where she received her Bachelor of Science degree in Accounting. After graduating from Tennessee State University, she relocated to Arizona to begin a career as a Financial Analyst for Raytheon, a fortune 500 company in the Aerospace industry. Early on in her career as a Financial Analyst, Ashlee became very successful receiving several awards and recognition for her performance and within a short period of time she was inspired to move up the corporate ladder to a Finance Manager. Inspired by her rapid growth and success, Ashlee decided she wanted to take her career and education a step further. She took a leap of faith, and requested a leave of absence from her position to pursue graduate school full-time. Ashlee was accepted to Virginia Commonwealth University (VCU) and relocated to Richmond, VA. She quickly learned graduate school was much different than her undergraduate experience and would cause her to become accustomed to navigating a fast paced environment. One key piece of advice Ashlee took with her when departing the doors of VCU is – it is okay to take different avenues to get to the same goal. There is no straight line in life and with every detour there is growth and lessons learned that will prepare you for more opportunities ahead. After graduating from VCU with a Master's of Science in Global Marketing Management, Ashlee relocated to Dallas, TX to continue working for the company where she began her Finance career and took on new responsibilities that include overseeing several corporate programs' budget and spending trends. Ashlee enjoyed her career in Finance, but after a couple of years back to work she realized something was missing. Working in her field ignited her passion to help others with their personal budget, taxes, and financial literacy. She longed for the client-relationships she experienced in her prior roles and after careful consideration and consulting of her mentors, she changed career paths and decided to re-enter the Accounting world. Since returning to the Accounting world, Ashlee has coached and provided financial consulting services to students, peers, business owners and aspiring entrepreneurs in the areas of tax liability, budgeting, expense tracking, reporting, and so much more. Currently, Ashlee works as a Tax Associate at Patterson, Hardee and Ballentine CPAs, a public CPA firm based in Franklin, TN. She is responsible for tax preparation and planning of high net-worth individuals and business clients with income revenues in excess of 1 million processing over 300 returns annually. Ashlee's desire to help others doesn't end with financial consulting, Ashlee is a proven leader and stays involved in the community as well as leads initiatives with the Tennessee State University National Alumni Association that include chartering two virtual alumni chapters and holding leadership roles within other local chapters. Ashlee continues to find ways to stay active with organizations that are dear to her, she is currently the lead author on a HBCU book project that highlights the work of various TSU Alumni, she has served as a panelist for Coins Over Gossip, a leadership development brand for Black Career Women and educated the attendees on what it takes to start a small business and tax impact. Although Ashlee has been successful in so many lanes, her greatest accomplishment is being a mother to her 4 and 6 year old.

KOEREYELLE DUBOSE

Do The Right Thing

Koereyelle Dubose

Attending Tennessee State University (TSU) was a no-brainer. After a campus tour (which happened to fall on a Wednesday), I was hooked! For anyone who has been to campus, you already know Wednesdays were always popping! As a high school junior who had only attended predominantly white schools, I was amazed to see how many positions of power my people held. Each office we toured was full of black faces. It felt like home.

In addition, I'd watched *Drum Line* two weeks before my tour and could imagine myself living my best life on campus.

When I arrived on campus in 2003, I had no idea how my life would transform based on how I spent the next four years. TSU raised me into the woman I am now. It provided me with the tools I needed to act toward my goals. It showed me that I was worthy of the things I said I wanted. It connected me to so many people who played a major role in my life.

TSU taught me so many things. Of all the life lessons, these four things really set the stage for the success I'm experiencing now.

#1 Being black is a gift, not a disadvantage.

Growing up as one of the only black students at my schools, it was easy to believe that being black was a disadvantage. We're taught that we must work harder, that we must show up earlier, stay later, and that we must be just a bit smarter than our white counterparts. At TSU, there was a leveled playing field for the first time in my life. I felt like my voice mattered, like I was understood and appreciated.

These days, I embody the TSU spirit in all that I do by educating black women of their potential and all the possibilities that await them *if* they pursue their life's purpose. My black pride was born in college, and I carry it with me to this day in all that I do.

One of the chief aims of my nonprofit, For the Culture Foundation, is HBCU advocacy and awareness, especially among students at predominantly white high schools. It's so important for our youth to understand the beauty and brilliance in their blackness. TSU definitely taught me that.

#2 There is so much power in your people.

One of the best blessings that comes from attending an HBCU is the family spirit. Since the campus isn't so big, everybody knows everybody, and you quickly learn that relationships (and your reputation) will make or break you.

TSU taught me the value of relationships. I learned how to establish, nurture and grow relationships that align with my goals. And, without TSU, many of the professional relationships that I now have would not be possible. I am connected to so many like-minded, like-spirited people because of my time at TSU. Two of the board members for my non-profit are TSU alums, Joscelyne Brazile and Marques Evans! That big blue connection is unmatched!

#3 When you surround yourself with excellence, you will excel.

You may have heard the phrase, "If you hang with four broke people, you'll be the fifth." That's real. At TSU, I learned the importance of surrounding yourself with excellence and adding value to your environment. But I also learned the importance of developing yourself so that you can add value and impact someone else.

It's pretty difficult to positively impact the life of someone else if you aren't constantly developing yourself. TSU taught me the importance of being a lifelong learner and finding joy in the journey of personal development.

#4 Nobody cares about your excuses; only execution matters.

I had the pleasure of attending TSU under the presidency of Dr. Hefner. He'd always start his speeches with this parable: "Every morning in Africa, a gazelle wakes up. It knows it must outrun the fastest lion, or it will be killed. Every morning in Africa, a lion wakes up. It knows it must run faster than the slowest gazelle, or it will starve. It doesn't matter whether you're the lion or a gazelle. When the sun comes up, you'd better be running."

Regardless of what's going on around us, we have to be laser-focused on what we are working toward. Regardless of what we "feel" like doing, despite our circumstances, we must show up ready to execute every single day in order to be successful.

I've taken the lessons learned at TSU, along with some learned the hard way through real-life experiences and used them to create my own university: *Werk University*. It is the first online trade school developed by a black woman, for black women. I'm on a constant mission to help change the lives of women around the world.

The work that I do, and the connection that I feel to my culture, would not be possible without my time spent at TSU. From wanting so badly to be a part of a community with *my* people, to being immersed in all things black, TSU was truly a dream come true. Without my time at TSU, where I learned to appreciate and celebrate all of my unique blackness, I don't know that I'd be willing to dedicate my life's work to our community.

To this day, I still connect with new people in new cities who have attended Tennessee State University. It's always an inexplicable embrace. I recently (and randomly) connected with someone from Jamaica at a dinner party who attended TSU. Her aunt is currently a professor there. There's no better way to break the ice than having "Big Blue" in common!

I am honored to be a part of this project. There's a special pride that comes from being part of the HBCU family. I truly feel blessed to have experienced the excellence of Tennessee State University, and I will forever advocate for it.

About Koereyelle Dubose

Koereyelle is a two-time author, award-winning entrepreneur and former educator who managed to turn her $32K teaching salary into a six-figure brand. She's the Founder of the 1st African American woman owned trade school in the country and is on a mission to connect women of color with the resources they need so they can stop living paycheck to paycheck.

She's an International Speaker, Podcast Host and Edutainer who's been featured nationally by Forbes, ESSENCE Magazine, The Huffington Post, NBC, TV One, VH1, Bravo TV and more for her empowerment projects.

Koereyelle is on a mission to help women uncover their purpose, prioritize their life and profit from their passions. Her motto is, "You already have everything you need to get everything you want, you just have to WERK for it."

.

ISAAC YAO ADDAE

Boomerang

Isaac Yao Addae

Who is Isaac Yao Addae? Simply put, I'm the physical manifestation of an immigrant's dream. My parents, born and raised in Ghana, West Africa, ventured to America in pursuit of something that had escaped them in their ancestral land. They followed a path similar to the transatlantic journey of our people generations before, albeit by aircraft and under their own free will, instead of by sea and through the brute force of enslavement. Their journey was grounded in the desire to gain opportunity, the chance to realize even the wildest of dreams. After all, that's what America was regarded as: the land of boundless opportunity.

While education has been the foundation of my family's socioeconomic ascent in America, much of what we've been able to accomplish can be credited to a single institution: the Historically Black College and/or University (HBCU). In order to gain the opportunities in which they desired, my parents understood the role of higher education as a critical element in their pursuit. Their journey to America started in Worcester, MA and eventually led them to Greensboro, NC, the town in which I was born. This is where my family first became introduced to the world of HBCUs.

My father, Dr. David Addae, earned his graduate degree at North Carolina Agricultural and Technical State University (N.C. A&T) by the time I was two years old. After completing his doctoral training at West Virginia University, our family ventured to the University of Arkansas at Pine Bluff (UAPB) where my father began his academic career as an assistant professor of industrial technology. He currently serves as a professor of advanced technologies at Alcorn State University in Lorman, MS.

My mother, Dr. Rejoice Addae, began her quest for higher education once our family settled in Pine Bluff. While raising three children and working full-time as an administrative assistant at UAPB, she enrolled in the undergraduate degree program in social work. Upon completion of her graduate degree in social work at the University of Arkansas at Little Rock, my mother spent several years working as a social worker in Arkansas and Mississippi. She eventually decided to pursue an academic career and taught in the social work department at Alcorn while she worked on her doctorate degree in social work at Jackson State University (JSU). She currently serves as a professor of social work at Arkansas State University in Jonesboro, AR.

Since both of our parents worked at HBCUs, my siblings and I spent a great deal of time immersed in the black college experience. Every summer, we were enrolled in just about every summer program on campus. We belonged to a group of professors' kids on campus that, seemingly, had free reign. During the summers, we'd wander around campus and engage with the college students who were there taking summer classes. We all felt at home. We were totally unaware of the fact that we were being nurtured by the HBCU environment throughout our formative stages, long before we became college students.

My parents, four of my siblings and I all have degrees from HBCUs. In addition, many family members that emigrated from Ghana eventually became HBCU alumni. So far, members of my immediate family possess undergraduate and graduate degrees from a total of eight HBCUs: Alcorn State University, Fisk University, Jackson State University, Morehouse School of Medicine, Morgan State University, North Carolina Agricultural and Technical State University, Southern University and A&M College, and Tennessee State University. I think it's safe to say that HBCUs played an integral role in my family's history, and no one should be surprised about how my journey has unfolded.

So, why did I choose to attend Tennessee State University (TSU)? My choice was initially all about the engineering programs. Coming out of high school, I was determined to attend a Southeastern Conference (SEC) University to study engineering. My father had been an HBCU professor since I was five years old, and I spent most of my life on HBCU campuses. But after campus visits, I had my mind set on attending Mississippi State

University or University of Tennessee since I'd been accepted to both. After talking to my father and my godfather, Dr. Napoleon Moses (former Alcorn provost), I realized the value that

HBCU engineering programs could offer. They told me that being a top engineering student of color at an HBCU was better than being that at a predominantly white institution. They had their reasons behind that logic. After that conversation, I started researching HBCU engineering programs.

One Thursday in May of 1999, while in Dr. Moses' office, he handed me the TSU academic catalog with the Aristocrat of Bands Sophisticated Ladies Band Dance Line on the front. I remember thinking how good the ladies looked. I said, "Now where's TSU located?" That was my first introduction to TSU. Up to that point, I was considering Florida A&M University (FAMU), Prairie View A&M University (PVAMU) and Howard University. I researched TSU online and saw that it was in Nashville, a city we visited annually because of Ghanaian family ties. I also read about the Engineering Concepts Institute (ECI) and saw that the application was due the following Monday. The next day, on Friday, I drove from Alcorn to the health department in Natchez to get my immunization records. Then, I pulled my application together. That afternoon, Dr. Moses drove me to Jackson, MS to ship off my application packet in time for it to reach TSU on Monday morning. From that point, my life was forever changed. I was eventually accepted to attend ECI in the summer of 1999.

During the ECI program, Dr. Decatur Rogers, the engineering dean at the time, took us to West Palm Beach, Florida to attend TechSymposium. It was a conference related to careers in technology. At the conference, I met Dr. Frederick S. Humphries, former FAMU and TSU President. He asked me about my high school GPA, my ACT score, and a few other questions. Afterward, he asked me to write down my mailing address. By the time I went back to Natchez after ECI, I had a full-ride scholarship, plus books, from FAMU. My mom asked me if I would go to TSU with 80% of the costs covered, or FAMU with 100% of the costs. It was a relatively easy decision for me. Being at TSU during ECI felt like I was at home. I had already built a bond with many friends, and the campus appealed to me more than any other campus I visited. I decided to attend TSU and I got work study to cover the remainder of the costs. I have absolutely no regrets!

Today, I'm thankful for Tennessee State University, an institution that changed my life! There's no other way to explain it. In June of 1999, I first visited TSU. Two months later, in August of 1999, I enrolled as a freshman electrical engineering student. By August of 2006, I had earned bachelor's and master's degrees from TSU's College of Engineering. My seven years as an engineering student were pivotal. Once I finished graduate school, I left Tennessee and ventured to Texas to start my career. By the time my engineering career ended, my resume reflected great experiences at some of America's well-known corporations such as Booz Allen Hamilton, CACI, Delphi Automotive, Ford Motor Company, IBM and Raytheon. I worked in many of the country's hottest markets, including Austin, TX; San Diego, CA; and the Washington, D.C. metro area. None of that would have been possible without my training at TSU.

After embarking on a corporate career in engineering, I decided to pursue my calling as a college professor. I began working on a doctorate degree in business administration at Morgan State University (a Maryland-based HBCU) while still working as an engineer. In 2015, my path led me to the role of assistant professor in TSU's College of Business, where I teach courses in business strategy, entrepreneurship and leadership. Like my days as a TSU engineering student, my life has been made better in my time as a TSU business professor. So many people poured into me while I was a student at TSU. In that same spirit, I now pour as much as I can into the students who I encounter each semester. I'll continue to embrace the university's motto, *Think. Work. Serve.* in my daily life. It is my hope to give TSU more than it gave me.

HBCUs truly do make a difference. They are one of the most important institutions in minority communities. TSU placed me on a path toward success at the ripe young age of 17. But prior to that, I had long been nurtured by HBCUs. The socioeconomic trajectory of my family has been heavily influenced by our varied HBCU experiences. It is my hope that my son, niece and nephews realize the immense value offered by HBCUs and earn at least one degree from one of these prized institutions (preferably TSU) in the future.

About Isaac Yao Addae

ISAAC ADDAE is a change agent dedicated to shifting the trajectory of individuals, communities & organizations. He earned a B.S. in Electrical Engineering and an M.S. in Systems Engineering from TSU. He is currently a Management Ph.D. candidate at Morgan State University's School of Business and Management.

As a corporate professional, Isaac gained 8 years of experience in technology consulting and systems development within an array of corporations (IBM, Booz Allen Hamilton, CACI, Raytheon). He is now an Assistant Professor in the College of Business at Tennessee State University (TSU) where he teaches courses in business strategy, entrepreneurship and leadership.

Purpose, influence and change are Isaac's core values, which he has exemplified through the establishment of initiatives that will continue to shift norms within communities of color. He has received numerous community recognitions, and actively serves a member of multiple nonprofit boards. Isaac considers fatherhood to be his greatest achievement.

***

.

CASSANDRA WILLIAMS

She's Got To Have It
Cassandra Holdsclaw Williams

Homecoming at an HBCU is more than indulging in a week-long binge of parties and events. It's certainly much more than a football game or catching up with old friends. An HBCU homecoming is a representation of black culture, legacy and pride. It's an annual tradition that reunites you with your alma mater. In 2018, Beyoncé gave us a glimpse of the HBCU experience with her epic two-hour performance at Coachella, paying homage to the HBCU homecoming tradition.

While homecoming is just one of many memorable experiences and benefits to attending an HBCU, it was an integral part of my HBCU experience. It made me proud of who I am and my black history. Attending homecoming each year inspires me to be my authentic self, even in environments where I'm the minority. It's the time of year where everything about who I am and what I love is celebrated because it was created with me in mind. Homecoming is a reminder of the things I appreciate the most about my childhood and growing up in my hometown.

I grew up in Inkster, Michigan, a small town outside of Detroit. The Detroit Metropolitan area is predominantly African American, and it has a rich musical history. It has also been a breeding ground for black activism and economic power. When you grow up in a place like this, there are many examples of black excellence. But it wasn't until I attended an HBCU that I recognized and appreciated my hometown and how I grew up.

I decided as a 17-year-old to move over 500 miles away from home and attend Tennessee State University. I experienced every emotion there is during that eight-hour drive to Nashville, Tennessee. I was excited, terrified and angry with my mom for pushing me to go. A week before leaving, I started doubting my decision and I was nervous about being so far away from home.

I was sad that I was leaving my close friends and family. I thought I had an idea of what to expect and what my experience would be like. However, I soon learned that idea didn't come close to my *actual* HBCU experience. The same girl who was terrified to leave everything that was familiar and live hundreds of miles away from home quickly found her independence and pieces of home at her beloved TSU.

As a high school student at Inkster High School, I had a sense of community and felt supported. I felt the same sense of community and support at TSU, but the difference was I wasn't considered as one of the best or the one on top. In high school, I excelled in everything.

I came from humble beginnings and was "the one who made it out." I stepped on Tennessee State University's campus very well decorated. I was Miss Inkster High School and I was homecoming queen. I was also at the top of my class academically. I was president of the student council, and I was the Track & Field MVP and the team captain.

When I arrived at TSU, I struggled my first year. Everyone was just as accomplished, if not more, than I was. While I felt supported, one of the hard truths I had to face was realizing that I may not be that same girl at TSU. As a freshman, for the first time in my life, I questioned if I was good enough.

The great thing about attending an HBCU is everyone is rooting for you. My professors challenged me, worked with me and created an environment for me to succeed. My friends inspired me to work hard and strive for greatness—not only with their words—but through their actions. I also observed their ambition and desire to be successful. I didn't only have my family back home encouraging me; I also had my TSU family right there with me every step of the way. I didn't have to look far for an example of excellence in my community. I was surrounded by black excellence every day. Only this time, I recognized and appreciated it.

One of the most memorable and exciting times of the school year at an HBCU is homecoming week. I did not grow up near any HBCUs and didn't know of any family members who attended an HBCU. So, TSU's homecoming was a new experience for me. It was like being a kid at Disney World for the first time. Every year, at the start of homecoming week, everyone would chant, "Get geeked! Get geeked! It's homecoming week. We don't go to class and we don't go to sleep. We stay up 24/7 the whole damn week." It was true. Our professors were even on board. They understood how meaningful this experience is for the students. Alumni will travel from all over the country to come back to what we refer to as our second home and support our alma mater.

Homecoming is an experience that stays with you. As TSU alumni, I think we appreciate homecoming more now than we did as students. I am still inspired when I attend homecoming festivities like the pep rally in the hole, the Battle of the Bands, Greek step show, tailgate, and the legendary half-time show. To see so many of my peers from my college days return to Nashville—people I haven't seen in years—it feels like a big family reunion. I'm always looking forward to hearing about their amazing careers and who they are now as husbands, wives, parents and professionals. I'm still in Nashville, still over 500 miles away from my hometown. The young freshman who questioned if she was good enough graduated from Tennessee State University with honors. She became a successful career woman and now helps other black women obtain the career of their dreams.

Homecoming reminds me of where I've been and how far I've come. We all have a story; we all come from different backgrounds and have different life experiences. However, when homecoming comes around, it's the one time each year that we all come together for the same experience. We come home to Nashville to connect with our TSU family. We show our pride, love and support for our university. We celebrate who we are and who we are yet to become.

About Cassandra Williams

Cassandra Williams is an experienced Human Resources leader with a background primarily within the healthcare industry contributing her HR expertise for both start-up companies and more established businesses. Cassandra is currently the Regional Human Resources Director for AdaptHealth, the 3rd largest provider of home medical equipment ("HME") in the country. She is also the founder of Career Talk With Cassandra, a career coaching brand dedicated to helping women find happiness and success in their careers as well as Coins Over Gossip, a leadership development brand for black career women.

Cassandra's educational credentials include, a Bachelor of Science degree in Psychology with a minor in Business Administration from Tennessee State University, and Master of Education in Organizational Leadership and Communication from Belmont University. In 2010, Cassandra obtained her Professional in Human Resources certification (PHR). Cassandra prides herself on being an innovative HR leader and strives daily to offer non-traditional, out of the box workforce solutions. Cassandra has many accomplishments, her work as a Career Coach and Blogger has been featured in Swagher.net "5 Keys to Interviewing Fearlessly" and "Finding your voice in the workplace." She was also featured on HR.com the largest network for HR professionals with over 250,000 members worldwide. Cassandra has been a speaker for Operation Stand Down (OSDTN), The Brentwood United Career Transition Support Group and Empowerment, Inc. She appeared as a guest on the Sistah Speak radio show 760 AM Gospel station as well as News Channel 5+, Urban Outlook.

FRANKLIN RIVERS III

He Got Game
Franklin D. Rivers, III

Some people have paths preset before them, while others figure it out along the way. Somewhere in the middle is where you find the lost.

The Tennessee State University, better known as TSU. How did I get there? It's a place I call home, where my entire era is family—not just my classmates. I fell in love with my HBCU during a spring day. I skipped school to kick it at Philander Smith College, my senior year in high school.

Everyone I kicked it with was going. I thought, *I'm not staying at school if y'all going.*

I didn't get the permission slip signed, so I left with everyone else who was headed to the bus and hopped in the whip. We jumped on Little Rock's I-630 to Philander Smith College for a college fair. I was just kicking it and having a good time. Little did I know, God ordained me to be a TSU Tiger. I *only* applied to TSU. However, I had never heard of it, or set foot on campus, and I wouldn't have been able to tell you that it was in Nashville until the spring of 2002. The alum at the table called for a group of us. We came over to them, listened, and filled out the free application. I had no plan after high school. I thought I was going to do what everyone else did: stick around, get a job and live my life. My bubble was Little Rock to Pine Bluff, Arkansas.

The phrase "HBCU" or "HBCU pride" didn't even register to me mentally. I grew up at University of Arkansas Pine Bluff (UAPB), and I was born in Pine Bluff. My parents are from Pine Bluff, although I was raised in Little Rock. UAPB was home, not an HBCU. This was my bubble, until I got a letter in the mail saying I was admitted to TSU. On the application, there is a line to list your major. I had no idea.

Two of my most impactful teachers were Ms. Iverson and Mr. Richardson.

Mr. Richardson was the geometry teacher who gave me problems that no one else had ever solved in his class. Ms. Iverson was the trigonometry teacher who talked me into taking calculus. I still don't know what I was thinking. Both of those teachers told me I was good at math and that I'd make a great engineer. Checkmark on the application! I'd major in engineering, even though I had no clue what I was getting myself into… Fake it until you make it, right?

I got accepted into TSU. High school graduation was approaching, and I still had no idea what I was doing with my life after I walked across that stage. I received a letter in the mail. It spoke about the Engineering Concepts Institute. The packet that introduced me to the force that is and forever will be Decatur B. Rogers. The letter said ECI, "*…was a five-week, residential, academic enrichment program that will be held on the main campus of TSU. The objectives of E.C.I. are to simulate the college experience, and to help prepare student participants for academic success, particularly in chemistry and math, in their first year of college.*" There was simply a $50 application fee and five weeks at Tennessee State University.

I yelled, "Mom, I wanna go to this if I get in!" since I didn't have any other plans that summer.

I accomplished so much during my time at TSU. I was a student-athlete (Flying Tiger), and I pledged Kappa Alpha Psi – Alpha Theta Chapter. I did plenty of service-learning and truly learned how to build the foundation of the man I am today because of TSU. It started with five weeks in the summer. I lived in Hale Hall with 49 of the coolest people I ever met. I also experienced some of the most laborious work I've ever done. But we had a lot of fun being nerds.

I never thought that what started as a five-week vacation would make me fall in love with TSU.

It was five weeks of statics, physics, navigating campus, hitting the café, working out in the game room, playing games, engineering field trips and making friends I have almost 20 years later. It was three weeks in when I knew that TSU is where I needed to be. I didn't even know it existed four months prior. I had no housing, no financial aid, no nothing. I had to scramble.

Here are a few things I learned by attending an HBCU:

1) How to hustle

2) How to circumvent when you get a "No"

3) How to find the backdoor when circumventing doesn't work

4) Where the connections are

5) When all else fails, start back at number one or pack to go home

During that summer, I went to Residence Life, my living… Watson… in a triple!

Nah, hell nah… I asked one of my summer classmates, "Psst! (with a head nod) Aye! How did you get in Hale for freshman year?" Doesn't hurt to ask.

The response? "Go talk your way into Honors or Friends of Honors." Dr. Jason Brewer, *life saver*! I ran around campus for the next two weeks between classes. Once I was done, I had a new dorm assignment, check. FAFSA, check. Now, time to wait for fall semester to start, check.

TSU Rites of Passage – Freshman Week: (1) The wait in The Forum for financial aid corrections, (2) registering for classes in Kean Hall, (3) trip to College Crib and (4) back to financial aid since my money had not posted. TSU became my home away from home, headaches to get things done, and all. There was no place I'd rather be than at TSU first semester.

I settled into what was comfortable for me. My routine was school, sports, sleep, and repeat in high school. I planned to do the same in college. I did track & field walk-on tryouts. Honors classes looked good on my transcript, so I took those. I even learned to spit a little game (I had zero in high school). The only thing I didn't count on was being in the honors program and it kicking me in the butt. I fooled around and took two classes that I had no business taking without knowing how to study—honors chem and advanced pre-cal.

There I was, sitting in the office with Coach Carter, trying to explain why the hell I had a "rounded-up" 2.0. Everything up until that point in my life came naturally. Academics, athletics, and even work/life balance. I didn't have to do anything extra. I didn't have to study before I got to TSU. I had a decision to make: learn how to study or learn how to move back home and figure out how to hide this until I got my grades back up. Two unexpected grades of D+ put a damper on my GPA real quick. I retook them both spring semester with better grades. TSU is a "grind" culture. Your environment keeps you grounded, no matter how hard you get knocked down.

This meeting defined the rest of my tenure at TSU. It took my head out of the clouds. Any NCAA athlete will tell you, 25-50-75. This means 25% of your credits must go toward degree completion by the end of your freshman year, 50% by your sophomore year, and so forth. Track & field was so ingrained in me that I could not stay at TSU without it. I had to make the grade with track & field or go home. I'm paying for this, well, these loans were. So, it was indeed a come to Jesus moment. Moments like this are what I love about TSU. There was always a moment that would shake your foundations, but we never let each other fall to the wayside. Without the Tennessee State University Track Frank, Kappa Frank, F Squared, M.B.A. Frank, HR Frank, or Coach Rivers does not exist.

If you saw me in undergrad, it appeared that I knew what I was doing— learning on the fly at its best. I was determined to find my path on my own. No matter where my path would take me, I would end up there on my terms, built with my will, and forged with all that I have. Then and now, when confidence or endurance is lacking, Tennessee State has and will always be my go-to foundation. To this day, if I'm silent or don't have much to say, I'm listening. I'm learning and building a toolkit for my next course of action. TSU taught me that you and you alone control your destiny as a continual work in progress.

Life is not perfect. I'm not perfect. My path isn't perfect. But without Tennessee State University, I have no idea where my path would have led me today.

About Franklin D. Rivers III

Franklin D. Rivers, III, a native of Little Rock, AR by way of Pine Bluff, AR is a proud alumnus of Tennessee State University where he received a B.S. degree in Interdisciplinary Studies concentrating on Biology and Psychology. After graduating from T.S.U., he remained in the Nashville area to work at a local Environmental Laboratory while being a volunteer coach at T.S.U. for two years. His time spent coaching lead to an M.S. in Sport Management and M.B.A. from Middle Tenn State University while working for Nelligan Sports Marketing acquired by Learfield Sports and Van Wagner Sports & Entertainment (VWSE). A friend suggested that he would be a good fit in the world of human resources due to his natural ability to coach & assess proper training/work environments. Franklin joined Nissan North America in 2013, working as an employee relations specialist for the next six years. In 2019, Franklin moved to the D.M.V. area to join American Airlines at a work environment investigator and giving back by volunteer coaching Track & Field at Howard University.

Franklin also holds an Ed.S. from MTSU; an H.R.D. focused graduate certificate in Diversity & Equity in Education and the highest coaching certificate given by USA Track and Field, and also the highest & diploma granted by the IAAF (International Association of Athletics Federations), now known as World Athletics.

.

MELODY HUBBARD-ROBINSON

Sister Act

Melody Hubbard-Robinson

It was a three-hour road trip to Tennessee State University (TSU). So many thoughts ran rampant through my mind in the car. *What if I don't fit in? What if I don't like it? Will I make any friends?* I thought of all of the things that could potentially make me call off this "going away to college" thing. Today, two TSU degrees later, I am grateful that I did not let fear talk me out of the biggest blessing of my life.

We got off at Exit 207 on Jefferson Street. As we made our way to 3500 John A. Merritt Boulevard, I saw a huge airplane. There were people everywhere. We pulled up to the freshman dormitory, Wilson Hall, affectionately known as "The Zoo." I got out of the car with my family and it was blissful chaos. The campus organizations were at the freshman dormitory to help us move in. They were even taking students to Wal-Mart and various stores. We were greeted with true southern hospitality.

After a few hours, everything calmed down … or so I thought. Out of nowhere, there was commotion outside the dorm. The ladies of Wilson hall came out of their rooms and headed outside. When we walked outside, all we heard was: "TS-TS-TS-TS-U ARIS-TO-CRAT, ARISTORCRAT OF BANDS, A-L-P-H-A, K-A-P-P-A, A-L-P-H-A, Alpha Kappa Alpha, Skeeeeeeeeeewwweeee, A-Phi-00006. Yo, baby Yo, OO-OOP." There were flashes of blue and white, pink and green, black and gold, and red and white. The band and Greeks were in full effect! I stood outside, thinking, *Oh, my God! It's A Different World!* The energy was wild, and the people were so welcoming. It was the biggest family reunion I'd ever attended. I knew in that moment that I was in a special place.

Suddenly, my fears were non-existent. I felt at home. I could breathe because I knew I could be exactly who I was called to be: *me.*

Land of Golden Sunshine

Tennessee State University shined the light of grace on me. One of the most remarkable advantages of attending an HBCU is the opportunity that they give students who cannot afford to spend a fortune on higher education. Additionally, they give students, like me (who did not score a 36 on the ACT) a chance at success. I attended TSU on a full scholarship. Knowing that my education was paid in full gave me the opportunity to direct all my energy to learning and successfully completing my classes.

I did not have the burden of paying tuition; however, the coursework was not a cakewalk. I had a plethora of challenging teachers. Even though I was not that fond of them at the time, upon graduation, I realized that they built my character and challenged me to adopt next-level thinking. They saw abilities in me that I didn't even recognize were inside me at the time.

During my freshman year, I accidently enrolled in Senior Level Biology instead of Intro to Biology for freshmen. I was completely lost. By the time I realized I was in the wrong class, it was too late to drop the class. I couldn't withdraw from the class, nor could I fail because both options would have forfeited my scholarship. So, I talked to the professor and she had empathy for me. She gave up her personal time to make sure I learned everything to pass her class. She tutored me outside of class and dedicated her office hours to help me with assignments. This level of commitment is none other than the HBCU experience. I passed the class with a B.

However, this was bigger than biology. It was a life lesson. I learned the significance of being in an environment that embraced people of color. I learned how vital it is to be willing to help someone when you have the tools, resources and power to do so. Importantly, I learned to pay it forward. At the Land of Golden Sunshine, you make an unofficial vow to support your fellow Tigers and black culture.

Double Major

I received both my Bachelor and Master of Business Administration from Tennessee State University. Business Administration was my "official" major, but if you've attended an HBCU, you "unofficially" had a double major in black excellence. Every class, building, dormitory, street and monument reinforced black pride and prestige.

We didn't only take the minimum required courses. We were challenged to take courses on African-American culture. We were not a small section in a history book. *Every month* was Black History Month. At an HBCU, black history, culture, leadership and entrepreneurship are core components of the curriculum. I was stretched to my maximum potential while at TSU.

I learned not to just do what is required—but to do what is necessary.

Shades of Black

Outside of an HBCU, many think that *black people* are all the same. Yes, it is obvious that we come in a myriad of beautiful shades of black. However, our skin tone is one minor difference in comparison to all the other areas of diversity among us. I was ignorant when I first arrived on campus. I, too, assumed that I would be around people just like me. I had no idea the amount of diversity on an HBCU campus.

People travel from all over the country to attend an HBCU. From up north to down south, from the east coast to west coast, every region was represented. I was amazed at how unique we are as a people. I was in awe at all of the accents and regional slang, not to mention all of the music I had never heard and the corresponding dances that went with that music. It was wonderful to be exposed to the beautiful shades of black.

The Annual Family Reunion

The bond does not end once you walk across the stage. The bond continues for a lifetime. At other universities, graduation is bittersweet. Everyone goes their separate ways oftentimes, and their paths may never cross again. However, if you were fortunate to attend an HBCU, it is not sad. You have something to look forward to each year: homecoming.

An HBCU homecoming is one tremendous family reunion. It is a production that includes vacation from work, new wardrobe and countless festivities. Imagine thousands upon thousands of graduates, along with their families and friends, flying in from all over the country. It's a weekend of reliving the excitement of campus life, celebrating HBCU pride, and creating new memories to cherish for a lifetime.

Power of Connection

One thing I have learned in this journey called life is that God works through people. While walking the campus, you know you are surrounded by greatness. However, you have no idea at the time that *greatness* would morph into *excellence*. Since we were challenged to go above and beyond, it's no surprise that we propelled to greater heights upon graduation. If you seize the opportunity to make fruitful connections, fast forward a few years and you will end up being connected to doctors, lawyers, politicians, educators, entrepreneurs, engineers, architects or even the "next big deal" story in *Essence* magazine! These connections become incredible resources. Whenever I am looking to collaborate on projects, seeking new opportunities, in need of guidance, or simply looking to connect with others on another level, I can access a plethora of fellow Tigers.

Wake Up Running

From the time you set foot on the campus, your mind is conditioned to have a winning spirit. Proudly singing the alma mater, joining campus organizations and countless hours of studying trained us to hit the ground running upon graduation. So, I will leave you with the famous quote that was branded in my heart—all of our hearts—throughout our matriculation at Tennessee State University:

"Every morning in Africa, a gazelle wakes up. It knows it must outrun the fastest lion, or it will be killed. The lion knows it must run faster than the slowest gazelle, or it will starve. It doesn't matter whether you're the lion or the gazelle. When the sun comes up, you'd better be running."

My HBCU experience taught me that, no matter what I wanted to be when I grew up, with strategy, hard work and excellence, I will always cross the finish line.

About Melody Hubbard-Robinson

Melody Hubbard-Robinson is the founder of Fierce Fearless Free Women Empowerment. (fiercefearlessfree.com) She is an international speaker whose captivating speeches inspire women across the world. She is the author of "No Bad B*tches Allowed," a call to action for women to be positive role models.

Receiving her Bachelors and Masters of Business Administration from Tennessee State University, Melody is the Human Resources Manager at a global company. She has a Professional HR Certification and is a SHRM Certified Professional. With over a decade of leadership, life and business coaching experience, Melody has helped women enhance their careers, build business, and maintain balanced lives.

Melody was accepted into the Forbes Coaches Council and was nominated for Memphis *Best in Black Awards* for Best Empowerment/Inspirational Brand. She has been featured in a plethora of publications. Additionally, she was a Memphis *Top 40 Under 40 Award* recipient and *Heroine Legacy Award* recipient.

.

HAROLD MOSES LOVE, JR. PHD

The Best Man

Harold Moses Love, Jr. PhD

When I think about my HBCU experience—specifically, *my experience* at TSU—I think about some of the happiest days of my life. My TSU experience began many years before I enrolled in college. My mother, Mary Y. Love, worked at TSU for 57 years, from 1956 to 2014. My mother spent ten years teaching mathematics and 47 years directing the TSU Upward Bound Program. As a result, I spent my summers and many days after school on TSU's campus. I enjoyed walking across campus and going into the band room to listen to the Aristocrat of Bands practice. All the while, I was dreaming of the day that I would be old enough to get into college and march in the band.

My father was a TSU alum, along with my mother. When I wasn't on campus with her,

I was at the state capitol with him, watching as he sponsored legislation, trying to make Tennessee a better state. Without fail, at some point during my visits to my father's office, the subject of TSU came up as he talked about his undergraduate experience. He explained to me how he was working to make sure TSU was included in the budget proposals for that year.

When I entered high school, my mind was already made up about where I was going to attend college. I did my best to prepare academically and I filled out my application with excitement. In August of 1990, I joined the list of Loves who attended TSU. My grandmother, Lillian Love, graduated in 1915 from Tennessee Agricultural and Industrial State Normal School. My father graduated from Tennessee Agricultural and Industrial State College. My mother graduated from Tennessee Agricultural and Industrial State University. My four sisters and I would graduate from Tennessee State University. In every evolution of TSU, there was a Love there. It seemed as if TSU was at the core of our family because our next-door neighbor was the director of financial aid, and the TSU chief of police was a member of our church. Growing up in this environment was a reminder of how HBCUs, like TSU, played such a crucial role in the lives of African Americans.

Some may ask if HBCUs are still relevant or needed with so many options for African Americans to attend college at predominantly white institutions. As I look back on my experience at TSU, I recall the unique experience of an HBCU for African Americans. When I started my freshman year, I was placed in the most diverse atmosphere I would be in for my entire life. I had traveled to Chicago, but never had a class and study group with someone from Chicago who could talk with so much passion about his hometown and why house music was so great. I never traveled to California; but when I met a young man from Vallejo, we became instant friends and later, fraternity brothers. Our conversations revealed that we had much in common as young black men seeking to improve ourselves intellectually. However, we had different life experiences because of the tensions between communities of color and the police in California.

I had the chance to sharpen my political skills as I managed two campaigns in a row for women who would be elected Miss TSU. Also, I worked behind the scenes to help the Student Government Association be successful. Those kinds of experiences can't be duplicated outside of HBCU campuses because of the unique experiences that every student brings to

The Yard. When I think about what HBCUs had to overcome to be established and still have their doors open, it is nothing short of a miracle. Being underfunded and expected to overcome obstacles that other institutions didn't have seemed to only make TSU and other HBCUs stronger. As a student, I knew the challenges that TSU faced because my father would tell me about his work at the capitol. Every time I saw TSU overcome them, I was encouraged to be a better student.

Are HBCUs still relevant and needed? Yes, they are! The world we live in still has young black men and women who need to be reminded of their greatness and have their potential molded. There are still young black boys and girls who need to hear about the discoveries being made by people who look like them and graduated from an HBCU. There are students who are not black who need to have black professors instructing them so they can go back to their communities with a different world view about diversity. That way, they will be able to affect change in ways that no one else can. There is a black graduate student who wants to be a college professor, but because of institutionalized racism, they may not get the opportunity that his or her degree should afford them. That professor needs an institution that will appreciate them for their academic worth and provide them the opportunity to educate the next generation of leaders.

If it wasn't for TSU, I wouldn't be where I am today. I came into TSU in 1990 as a freshman with a less than clear vision of what I wanted to do in life. Over the next four years, I became a member of the Aristocrat of Bands and I was initiated into the Mighty Rho Psi Chapter of the Omega Psi Phi Fraternity. I developed lifelong friendships and I am committed to helping the university in any way I can. When I got elected a state representative in 2012, TSU was included in my legislative district. I had the opportunity to continue my father's work of advocacy for TSU at the capitol. But the greatest thing TSU gave me was my marriage in 2019 to my wife, Leah, who is a TSU alum, as well.

About Harold Love, Jr. Ph.D

Harold M. Love., Jr. is a Nashville native and TN State Representative for the 58th Legislative District. He serves on the following Committees in the TN House of Representatives: Education, State Government, Consumer and Human Resources, and Tennessee Advisory Council on Intergovernmental Affairs.

Love is a member of the Omega Psi Phi, Fraternity, Inc., a 33° Mason, Shriner and Board Member of the 18th Avenue Family Enrichment Center.

Love received his Bachelor's in Economics and Finance with a minor in Political Science and Ph.D in Public Policy and Administration from Tennessee State University, and a Masters degree is Theological Studies from Vanderbilt University School of Divinity.

Love was ordained an elder by the A.M.E. Church in 1999 and currently serves as the pastor of Lee Chapel A.M.E. Church.

Love resides in Nashville with his wife, Leah.

.

LEAH DUPREE LOVE, ESQ

Poetic Justice
Leah Dupree Love, Esq.

My blood runs blue. I say that because, for the last 70 years, a member of my family has attended Tennessee State University (TSU). I began my matriculation at TSU in the fall of 2001. On one of my trips home from school, I stopped by my paternal grandmother's house. She had a box waiting for me. In that box were memorabilia she kept from her freshman year, including tickets to athletic games she never attended. That visit reminded me of my family's legacy with HBCUs, the importance of faith, and our commitment to education.

I was born in Jackson, Tennessee, and my high school sits directly across the street from Lane College, another HBCU. My father and several other family members attended

Lane College, including my paternal great-grandmother and her sister. They were salutatorian and valedictorian of their graduating class when the institution was only a high school. I knew I wanted to leave Jackson, but I wanted to attend an HBCU. Even more family members attended TSU and I had an older cousin who was currently attending. I am one of those people who sets my mind on a target and will do anything to achieve it. As such, I went on one college tour and applied to only one school: TSU. I still do not know how my parents allowed me to do that. However, there was no doubt in my mind that I would be accepted. Not only was I accepted, but I received a full-ride, Presidential Scholarship.

Oftentimes, students come to HBCUs broken and in search of a new identity. TSU is one of those schools that takes the charge to educate black students seriously, while building on its heritage and preparing leaders for a global society. For most, going away to college is the first opportunity you have to make your own decisions. You decide when you will wake up in the morning and how you will spend your day. It is a time of uncertainty and fear. However, I never felt uncertain or afraid when I got to TSU. Everyone around me looked like me, dressed like me, liked the things I liked and laughed at the things I found funny. It was a safe space to express doubt, frustration and happiness. It was *home*.

I quickly found myself immersed in college life. I joined clubs and societies, participated in the *Honda* College Bowl, represented several countries at the United Nations, and became a member of Alpha Kappa Alpha Sorority, Incorporated, Alpha Psi Chapter. One of the most rewarding opportunities I received from TSU was securing an internship at the state capitol. Little did I know that internship changed the trajectory of my career and further ignited my passion to help others.

After graduating, I moved to Indiana for graduate school and law school. For as long as I can remember, I wanted to become a sports agent and represent athletes. While I loved the job at the NCAA, I was not fulfilled. One day, I decided to leave and move back to Nashville. It was as if something was calling me back. I came back to campus every year for homecoming and donated to the foundation, but nothing I was doing in Indiana made me feel as alive and needed as when I attended TSU. I made a call to the intern director at the state legislature I had while at TSU. I explained to her I was a former intern and wanted to "come back home." She connected me with the Tennessee Senate, where I served as a clerk and legislative aide for two years before joining the governor's office as director of legislation for the Department of General Services. I served in that role for six years.

I met my husband, State Representative Harold M. Love, Jr. while working at the legislature. We met because he and my sister attended TSU at the same time, and she told me to look out for him after he was elected. We instantly connected over our shared experiences of Greek life, Wonderful Wednesdays and homecoming. Although several years separated us as students, the spirit of TSU lives within each person who enters her doors. My husband's family legacy at TSU spans several generations to include two Miss TSUs. We both understand TSU is a breeding ground of excellence, fertilized by the blood, sweat and tears of those students who initially attended Tennessee Agricultural & Industrial State Normal School for Negroes. We are more than committed to the financial, academic and administrative stability of TSU, and we can only hope our children find comfort in the legacy we have created.

After I left state government, I opened my own law practice. Eleven months later, TSU President, Dr. Glover, called me to see if I wanted to work at the university because I was an alum. I also possessed a particular set of skills needed to help lobby for the needs of TSU at the state legislature. I was always taught that we all have a duty to serve and give back to the people, and the community that helped shape you. I was honored and excited to take on my new role as director of government relations. Working at TSU, or even for the government, was never my plan. However, TSU has a way of cultivating untapped abilities and developing leaders.

My personal mission is to put God's love in action by leading a life built on helping and serving others, inspiring hope in the least among us, and using my gifts to encourage others to live their best lives. Every job and volunteer commitment I have considered has been centered on this mission statement. Years from now, when someone mentions my name, I want them to say, "She cared." I want to be someone who made my community better because of my commitment to service. I want to be in charge of how and when I help others and have a career with the flexibility to help more people.

TSU taught me that it is more than just a bachelor's degree or a current place of employment. I learned who I was, what I wanted and what really mattered. I became better, wiser and stronger the moment I stepped on campus. I entered to learn and left with a greater passion to serve.

My blood runs blue.

About Leah Dupree Love, Esq

Leah Dupree Love serves as the Government Affairs Officer for Tennessee State University. In her role, she assists the President and university leadership with communication to state and local government officials regarding policy and program issues facing the institution. Also, Mrs. Love owns Dupree Consulting Group where she assists clients with business formation and succession, and various other legal matters.

Previously, Mrs. Love has served as Director of Legislative Services for the Tennessee Department of General Services and an Adjunct Business Law Professor at Tennessee State University.

Mrs. Love is a member of several organizations and boards, including Alpha Kappa Alpha Sorority, Inc., Hendersonville Area Chapter of The Links, Incorporated, Advisory Board Chair of YMCA Community Action Programs of Middle Tennessee and Advisory Board Vice Chair of Tennessee State University Accounting.

Mrs. Love received her Bachelor's degree from Tennessee State University; a Masters in Business Administration from Valparaiso University, and a Juris Doctorate from Indiana University Robert H. McKinney School of Law.

Mrs. Love is a member of Lee Chapel AME Church where her husband, State Representative Harold M. Love, Jr. is the Pastor.

.

ALFRED DEGRAFINREID II

Coming to America
Alfred Degrafinreid II

In my opinion, Historically Black Colleges and Universities (HBCUs) are the equivalent of Wakanda from the popular film, Black Panther. HBCUs expose students to the highest levels of excellence and provide them with appropriate life skills in preparation for success in mainstream society. Some of the sharpest minds and most skilled athletes gained their foundational wisdom from this rich institution since its inception as Tennessee Agricultural & Industrial State Normal School for Negroes in 1912. In 2020, Tennessee State University (TSU) is still cultivating a culture of excellence where we, "Think. Work. Serve."

My family's TSU story began in the mid-1960s when my uncle became the first member of my family to attend college at Tennessee A&I. He could have easily participated in the black migration out of the rural south to the Midwest, like his older siblings. Alternatively, he could have been drafted to fight in the Vietnam War. It is hard to imagine the pressures that a first-generation college student felt in the 1960s—or any time, for that matter. But it is particularly difficult when you have eleven siblings. The pressure was immense because familial resources were scarce, and failure was not an option. He had to be a role model for his younger siblings—one of which was my mother. She became the first female in our family to attend college at TSU in 1973.

My first memory of TSU's campus began nearly 20 years after my mom first arrived on campus. My brother graduated from high school in 1993, and I was excited to help him move into his dorm at Watson Hall. It was only fitting to help him move because, when he graduated, I now had a room to myself. This was my first chance to connect the dots from what I had seen on

A Different World (a spin-off of The Cosby Show). This set the stage for our new normal with a sibling now in college.

I vividly remember the drive from Memphis to Nashville. My mother insisted that we stop at Ed's Catfish for a fish sandwich before going to campus. I remember my first walk through the brand-new Floyd-Payne Student Center—especially when we proceeded to the basement to visit the Student Recreation Center. I was in paradise because there was a

Street Fighter arcade game, pool tables, a bowling alley and a group of students playing Spades. My mom drove from Nashville to Memphis and cried for the entire three-hour drive back home.

A couple of weeks later, we scored tickets to the Southern Heritage Classic, which is always held in Memphis at The Liberty Bowl. I remember the tailgating, loud music, smoked turkey legs and, most of all, the halftime show. Visiting the campus and attending the football game in the fourth grade changed my perspective on my educational goals, especially since many people from my zip code in North Memphis (38127) did not go to college.

My sister was accepted into TSU in the fall of 1999. But it was more difficult moving her into Wilson Hall. I imagine that my sister was underwhelmed when she heard that her dorm was commonly called "The Zoo." As a high-school student, I was anxious to walk around campus because I knew that college was within my reach. As a teenager, I was particularly interested in attending step shows, the Battle of the Bands and the homecoming concert.

In the spring of 2001, I received an acceptance letter to TSU on a full academic scholarship (also known as The Presidential Scholarship). My family had greatly benefited from receiving degrees from this fine institution of higher education. I was pleased that I would be added to that number.

I was encouraged to apply to the Packard Science Institute Summer Program, which was geared toward incoming students majoring in math or science. I was undecided on my major going into college. This must have been the precursor to what we hear about today with STEM and STEAM initiatives. This cohort was life changing. I was connected to smart students

76

from across the nation—many of whom now have degrees in business, engineering, medicine and law.

Politics

My interest in electoral politics began in middle school. I was an officer on the Student Government Association (SGA) through high school, so I thought it would be a natural progression to continue SGA in college. There were two freshmen positions on SGA. I ran unsuccessfully for one of them, losing by eleven votes. My campaign strategy was flawed. I figured that males were outnumbered by females 20:1, so there was no need to campaign in the male dorms. I also relied on the fact that I was from Memphis and that my hometown would automatically vote for me. Big mistake. I learned a valuable lesson on political strategy after that loss. I redeemed myself and was subsequently elected to the House of Delegates for both my sophomore and junior years of college.

The SGA and the Royal Court always traveled together to help the Office of Admissions recruit students in the cities where TSU played football. I was heavily recruited by the

Speech-Pathology Department during a visit to Memphis for the Southern Heritage Classic weekend. That's when I finally declared my major. I enjoyed learning about the acquisition of language, the brain, the articulators and hearing. Speech Language Pathology and Audiology was no joke! The professors, in large part, were no-nonsense teachers. I had an ethereal experience in 2005 due to an extra credit assignment. Our professors encouraged us to visit the Tennessee General Assembly for our profession's lobby day on The Hill. I immediately fell in love with the legislative process.

I honed my political skills once I was initiated into the Alpha Theta Chapter of Kappa Alpha Psi Fraternity, Inc. in the spring of 2004. I received an honorary Doctor of Politics through my involvement with the fraternity. I experienced just as many wins as I did losses—but I wouldn't change the process. I met Senator Thelma Harper on campus, and I asked her to teach me about politics. She invited me to lunch and connected me with the person who provided me with my first internship. I got to shadow the lobbyist for the Tennessee State Employees Association during legislative session and saw firsthand how bills become law.

My first professional job outside of college was working for a TSU alumnus and a frat brother, Vice Mayor Howard Gentry. Mr. Gentry took me under his wing on his 2007 bid for Nashville mayor. During my interview for the job, Mr. Gentry told me that he could not run for mayor without having an HBCU graduate working with him each day. But his preference was to have a TSU graduate on his staff. He paid it forward by teaching me local politics. The exposure that I received from that job played a substantial role in securing future job opportunities on the local, state and federal levels of government. While working the campaign, I enrolled in the Master of Public Administration program. I gained so much more than an education in the program; I gained the confidence to continue into a Doctor of Jurisprudence program at Indiana University.

Following professional school, I have had more great opportunities than I ever could have imagined. And I'm proud to say, I've been successful in those roles. I have advised councilmembers, constitutional officers, mayors, legislators, governors, congressmen and college presidents in multiple states. I have served on national boards and even as chairman for a multitude of nonprofit boards in Middle Tennessee.

The foundation that I received from TSU was second to none. As I look back over my life, I often engage in the "nature vs. nurture" analysis. Am I who I am today because of some innate capability, or because of the people who poured into me over my lifetime? I have been nurtured by many people, and a large portion of those same people had their minds shaped at Tennessee State University.

I would be remiss, however, if I did not mention that I met my wife in graduate school at TSU. More than 13 years later, we have celebrated seven years of marriage and the birth of two children. You can usually find us mentoring students at TSU and attending TSU functions regularly. Our children can be seen wearing "Future TSU Tiger" t-shirts throughout town.

We entered TSU to learn. Today, we have gone forward to serve. Go Big Blue!

About Alfred Degrafinreid II

Alfred Degrafinreid II currently works for Vanderbilt University in the capacity of Associate Vice Chancellor for Community Relations, where he directs both local government and community engagement for the university.

Degrafinreid has managed and advised several local, state and federal political campaigns, as well as worked in senior level positions on the local, state and federal levels of government.

Degrafinreid attained the Bachelor of Science and Master of Public Administration degrees from one of the greatest HBCU's in the land, Tennessee State University. He also attained the Doctor of Jurisprudence degree from Indiana University Robert H. McKinney School of Law.

A native Tennessean, Degrafinreid was born in Memphis to Patricia and the late Alfred Degrafinreid, Sr. He is married to Tiffany (Jones) Degrafinreid and they have two children, Alfred III (4) and Chancellor Joelle (2).

.

MADELYN HUBBARD

School Daze

Madelyn Hubbard

College wasn't optional for me. My mother always instilled the importance of going to school and getting a good education. When I entered my senior year of high school, my dream of going off to college one day became more real than I could have ever imagined. I wanted to go far away. In fact, my dream was to attend a university in California. I didn't know anything about California or colleges in that area. All I knew was that I wanted to move to California. Fortunately, that wasn't God's plan for me. Little did I know that those brief moments of disappointment would set me up for what was about to be the best days of my life. At the time, I didn't know that college wasn't just about going to class and learning the curriculum. It was going to be a learning experience for all aspects of my life. I am who I am today because I was accepted into the best HBCU in the land: Tennessee State University.

The first day I arrived on the TSU campus, I experienced a whirlwind of emotions!

I was scared, excited, anxious and nervous all at the same time. So many questions ran through my mind. *Will I like it here? Will I make friends? How am I going to live so far away from my mama?* My high school days were over. I was about to embark on this new journey and didn't know what to expect! Growing up in Tennessee, I thought I knew everything about TSU.

I went to the Southern Heritage Classics every year and I had always heard of the *epic* homecoming events. That was just the surface. TSU is so much more than that.

My experience didn't start in Wilson Hall, or "The Zoo" as many people called it. I was assigned to Eppse Hall, which made me nervous. I was already uneasy about living away from home with girls who I didn't know, but now I was also in a dorm with upperclassmen. I had planned to be roommates with my friend from high school in Wilson Hall. Although I was disappointed in the fact that we wouldn't be roommates, it didn't take away from the first day in the Land of Golden Sunshine. However, it worked out in the end. My friend and I went to Wilson and requested to be roommates. Not only did they approve it, but I ended up in the same room as my sister in Wilson Hall, Room 141. That made me so happy.

When I walked around campus, I noticed all the sororities and fraternities strolling and helping the freshmen move in. I felt like a child. I was so fascinated with the lovely ladies of Alpha Kappa Alpha Sorority, Incorporated yelling, "Skeeee Weeee!"; the men of Alpha Phi Alpha yelling, "A-Phi!"; the pretty boy Nupes of Kappa Alpha Psi yelling, "Yo, Baby! Yo, Baby, Yo!"; the ladies of Delta Sigma Theta yelling, "OOOOPPP!"; those country boys of

Phi Beta Sigma yelling, "Blue Phi, You Know!"; and, of course, the ladies of Zeta Phi Beta yelling, "Z Phi!" Even the ones who were moving in were dressed to a T. Some even had on suits. At my age, I didn't see many people around me dressed like that unless we were at church or at a special program. I was walking around in sweats, my high school letterman jacket, with a ponytail. It was official. I was in a different world.

At freshmen orientation, I looked around the room and realized I was with people from all over the world. They told us, "Look to your left and look to your right. One of the people next to you won't be there with you in four years." *Would I be that one person?* That was a scary thought. I listened to all the accents in the room. I heard so many accents from down south, the west coast, the east coast, up north and even international. The phrases that I had never heard before until I stepped foot on campus still crack me up to this day. The two in particular that I remember most were, "Aye, shawty!" and "What up, doe?" All of these students from all over the world had come all the way to Tennessee just to go to school. I originally was trying to get as far away from Tennessee as possible. I guess they knew something I didn't.

Fast forward to the first day of class. I will never forget freshman orientation class with Dr. Elsie. He was so serious about learning the alma mater. I didn't realize at the time that I would appreciate that so much. Every time I get a chance to sing it, I sing it with great pride and joy. In the Land of Golden Sunshine by the Cumberland's fertile shore. I attended a school with greater service, one that I will always adore. My dear alma mater, how I love thee, love thy white and blue. May I strive to meet thy mandates with faith that's true.

I'd made it to my first Wonderful Wednesday. Who knew a typical Wednesday would be a fashion show, day party and cookout all at the same time? When I toured the campus, I was advised not to schedule classes around lunch on Wednesdays. I now understood why. I would have been devastated to miss that experience. There was music, chanting, and Greeks filling the campus. I don't think I missed a Wonderful Wednesday in all my four years on campus.

"Get geeked! Get geeked! It's homecoming week! We don't go to class and we don't go to sleep. We stay up 24/7 the whole week." The rumors of TSU's homecoming didn't do it justice. The week started off with the Alpha caravan, an experience I will never forget. Then, there were parties, the pep rally and, of course, the big game. Nashville was packed to capacity. People traveled from all over to attend TSU's homecoming.

Sophomore year was just as amazing as my freshman year. In just one short year, I was no longer that same girl from Memphis. I had grown into a young woman. I was more involved on campus and enjoyed all the benefits of attending an HBCU. By this point, I had met Jesse Jackson, Judge Hatchett, Linda Brown from the *Brown versus Board of Education*, Malcolm X's daughter, Freedom Riders and Dick Gregory. I made it a point to attend all the forums with our civil rights heroes. This was an experience that I wouldn't have received at a predominantly white institution. My history teacher was actively involved in a lot of the civil rights movements in Nashville. My history lessons weren't from a book, but from personal stories and experiences of my professors. Coming from a family rich in black history and civil rights involvement in Memphis, this was amazing for me. I loved every moment of it. I also became more active in the NAACP. I went on to be Miss NAACP, then the president of my chapter.

More than any other year, junior year was most memorable. This was the year that I pledged the Awesomely Sophisticated Alpha Psi Chapter of the first and finest sorority, Alpha Kappa Alpha Sorority, Incorporated. I am a member of the sorority that I had dreamed of all my life. I also became a member of Phi Beta Lambda Business Fraternity. You couldn't tell me anything. I didn't think things could have gotten any better. As a senior, I had mixed emotions. I tried to take a double major because I wasn't ready to leave TSU. I begged and pleaded with my mother, crying, "No, I don't want to leave." It was a sad moment for me! The fear of leaving my comfortable community to enter the real world alone was scary. I had gained so many friends that would be in my life forever. It just killed me inside that my best years were about to end.

On May 3, 2008, it was graduation day. As excited as I was, I was still sad. Although my college life was only four short years, what I gained from that experience will stick with me for the rest of my life. Each year, I look forward to going back to homecoming, which is now more like a family reunion for me. That is my one week every year that I get to relive the best years of my life with people who I love so dearly. TTT-SSS -U, I will always love you!

About Madelyn Hubbard

Madelyn "Maddie Cakes" Hubbard is a "Culinista" at heart. With a Bachelor's in Business Management from Tennessee State University, she always knew that she would be the owner of her own dessert and catering business.

June 2008 in Nashville, TN, she opened Madelyn's Creations, inspired by her love and passion for baking. In January 2017, she decided to re-brand making all things DAINTY. She launched her business in Houston, TX. "Baked with a DAINTY twist!" Her culinary platform includes My Dainty Dish, My Dainty Cakes, and now introducing My Dainty Dipped.

My Dainty Dish includes catering and a video series on YouTube. Madelyn is also a published author of two cookbooks entitled "My Dainty Dish Healthy Summertime Cookbook" and "Soulful Favorites".

My Dainty Cakes is known for its creative cupcake collections, custom cakes, and it's "dainty" twist on traditional delectable treats.

Launched January 2020, My Dainty Dipped specializes in fruit bouquets and arrangements.

SAMUEL BROWN III

Higher Learning
Samuel Brown III

When it came time for me to apply to colleges, Tennessee State University was not my first choice. Twenty-five years ago, my father became the professor of aerospace studies at AFROTC Detachment 790. Not long after finding out we were moving to Nashville, my sister was killed in a car accident. My world changed forever. But, little did I know, moving to Tennessee was just the fresh start my family needed. My mother accepted a job at Vanderbilt, and I started school at Martin Luther King, Jr. Academic Magnet High School.

My parents had very demanding work schedules. I often found myself doing homework at their offices after school or hanging out while I waited for my dad to get off work. Occasionally, a cadet was assigned to tutor me or take me around campus for "academic inspiration." A lot of those study sessions were cut short by my inability to focus due to the laughter and shouting coming from the game room, or the sound of basketballs on Kean Court. As the years passed, I found myself spending more time immersed in the "Big Blue" culture. When I was not in tutoring with a cadet, I could be spotted at various homecoming events, step shows, football games (in the hole), basketball games and concerts in Gentry Center, in addition to various summer engineering programs.

My family moved back to the DMV (the D.C. metro area composed of D.C., Maryland and Virginia) my junior year in high school. I dreamed of becoming an NCAA Division I athlete, and I wanted to be a pilot, too. I learned I could do both by attending the United States Air Force Academy in Colorado Springs, Colorado. I ultimately received an appointment as a member of the Class of 2006, but quickly realized that life at USAFA was difficult.

I was away from home and I had little support system. I was in an environment unlike any I'd ever experienced. I struggled to keep up with

89

the rigorous academic curriculum. To make matters worse, I lost two of my closest friends to street violence that fall.

In the end, on a snowy day in March 2002, I was dismissed from the academy and honorably discharged from the Air Force Reserve for "failure to adhere to academic and military standards." Like any 18-year-old, I felt like life as I knew it was over. I squandered a tremendous opportunity and had nothing to show for eight months of effort. I'm not proud to admit this, but I resigned myself to spending the next few months feeling completely sorry for myself. I spent a lot of time rationalizing my failure, with no plan to pick up the pieces. It wasn't long before I found myself self-destructing. I realized I was nowhere near my intended purpose or potential. I forced myself to analyze why the academy experience went so wrong and why my life was so far off its intended track.

I realized I didn't make it at USAFA because I didn't really want it. I felt the need to impress my parents and my family, but it wasn't the right place for me. I couldn't fake my way through that, no matter how hard I tried. In a last effort to do something, I enrolled at North Carolina State University. I attended classes for two days and caught the first train back to D.C.

I refused to make the same mistake twice; NC State wasn't for me, either.

I reached out to my father and asked if he could pull some strings to help me get back into TSU. The fall semester had just begun, and I was way behind the curve. I couldn't stay in D.C. Luckily, Dean Cade, Dr. Hefner, Dean Rodgers, Dr. Holt and Dean Earnest went out on a limb to help me. They took a chance on me. As much as I'd like to tell you I had learned my lesson and hit the ground running, that would be the furthest thing from the truth. I completely let every one of them down almost immediately. I managed to get kicked out of Hale Hall and ended my freshman year with a 1.8 GPA.

Like many in my demographic, I've been counted out and marginalized on countless occasions. At times, I found myself criticized by the very people who were placed in positions to help prepare me for the world. At times, the educators and the very system that existed around me conditioned me to believe I could not, and would not, amount to anything. Thankfully, this was not the case at TSU.

Dean Rodgers once taught me that I was God's idea and heaven's dream. He reminded me that the universe I came to exist in had already empowered me to be so; I just hadn't realized it yet. Over the next four years, I met some of the most amazing people who were seeking various degrees to empower them for the best possible start for the next stage of their lives. That truly inspired me. Those inspirations became friends. Some became fraternity brothers, while others became memories. We were all part of a community of ideals set in motion by past alumni who expected to exceed their wildest dreams and leave an indelible mark on this world.

On August 12, 2006, 29 months after the Air Force debacle, my parents pinned two gold bars on my shoulders as I was commissioned as a 2nd Lieutenant. I received an allocation to attend flight school, and my ceremony took place in the one of the rooms I used to do my homework in. I'd come full circle. It was in that moment that I knew I could do anything I put my mind to.

In my opinion, one of the most powerful tools we have at our disposal is our mindset.

For instance, consider the hashtag #opportunityisnowhere. Some will see the hashtag and read it as, "Opportunity is nowhere." But adjusting our mindset and perspective accordingly, one might see the message also reads, "Opportunity is now here." The TSU experience helped me to shift my mindset to the latter. That shift enabled me to become a product of an environment that produced the likes of Jesse Russell, Oprah Winfrey, Lloyd 'Fig' Newton, and countless others.

TSU may not have been my first choice, but it taught me that failure doesn't make one a loser. Quitting doesn't make one a coward, and vulnerability doesn't make one weak. It takes courage to try new things. Bravery is embracing vulnerability and acting despite fear. I hope TSU continues to empower future generations to look at the glass as half-full and not take, "No" for an answer. If there is no door available to your dream, find a window. If there is no window, find a vent. If there's no vent, get a shovel and start digging. Find a way, make a way, to be where you want to be.

Thank you for everything, Tennessee State University! Thank you for saving my life!

About Samuel Brown III

Samuel Brown III, a native of Prince George's County Maryland, is a proud alumni of Tennessee State University where he received a B.S. in Aeronautical & Industrial Technology in 2006. After graduating from TSU, Sam commissioned as a 2nd Lieutenant in the United States Air Force and attended Combat Systems Officer training at Randolph AFB, Texas. After a year of flying training, he decided to pursue Aircraft Maintenance to gain more experience in the leadership and management of people. He deployed in support of Operation Enduring Freedom in Afghanistan, Operation Unified Response in Haiti, and Operation Iraqi Freedom. In 2010, Sam became the youngest Senior Manager in the history of Boeing Commercial Airplanes while continuing to serve as an Air Force Reservist. During his time with Boeing Company, he helped to establish the 787 Dreamliner facility in Charleston South Carolina and led lean manufacturing practices that delivered the first 100 airplanes from Charleston. In 2016, Sam was recruited to lead the Custom Fabrication operation at TAIT, the world's leading entertainment manufacturing company. He currently serves as the Vice President of Global Operations and is responsible for all Business Systems, Global Process Alignment, Fabrication, Production Support, Safety, Quality and Facilities functions for the company. In his personal life, Sam is the father of a 13 year old daughter and a four year old son. He is active in community outreach and educational enrichment for underrepresented youth. Lastly, Sam started his own production management consulting firm with active contracts that aim to assist businesses in achieving leaner operations that yield revenue and margin consistency.

Sam also holds a M.S. degree in Operations Management from the University of Arkansas and is currently pursuing a EdD in Organizational Leadership.

JUAN ADAMS

Boyz In The Hood

Juan Adams

My path to the HBCU experience was a little different than most. Pursuing a college education was *never* a part of *my* plans. Reflecting, that decision could seem ironic, given that my mother was a Tennessee State University graduate and was immensely proud of her alma mater. Her closest friends, to this day, are her TSU classmates, who represent 40 plus years of friendship. With that collegiate influence presented to me, the thought of following in her footsteps never crossed my mind.

My original plan was to join the military—not because of my personal passion—but because of my aunt's influence. She vowed that joining the military was the best path for me in order for me to become a successful, young black man. After several outings and bonding with my recruiter, my mind was set on the Navy—*or so I thought*. When the day came for me to take my military physical, my guidance counselor encouraged me to speak with the ROTC teacher about the pros and cons of the joining the military. Learning that I would be away from my family for extended periods of time while living on a ship was enough to kill my short-lived dream. That conversation altered my path and my track.

After graduating high school, I had no direction. I continued to work my part-time job through that summer. During that summer, my close friend participated in a program that helped him prepare for his college transition at Tennessee State University (TSU). After visiting him, I was instantly intrigued while I was on campus. Most significantly, I noticed that everyone there looked like *me*. My interest grew more when we visited the Student Center. There were TV rooms, the bookstore, a gym and a game room all under one roof. But my favorite spot was the food lounge known as "The Sub." The Sub had Burger King, Taco Bell and Pizza Hut all in one setting. I never imagined spending so much time in this one place would create so many memories. I became more interested in attending college. The icing on the cake was my visit to his residence hall.

My friend's room was set up with his TV, gaming system, cookware and clothes. At that point, I didn't just see college; I saw freedom! Convinced that enrolling into TSU would award me these things, plus an education, I was sold! If TSU was good enough for my mom, TSU would be good enough for me.

What I wasn't prepared for was the enrollment process. Registering four weeks prior to school starting was like putting a puzzle together with all the wrong pieces. That month felt like I lived in the financial aid office. During that time, I built a strong relationship with a staff member, who advocated for my successful enrollment. This allowed me to contact her directly for assistance to avoid the long lines. Financial aid? Check! Unfortunately, it was too late in the registration process to obtain housing. The dormitories were *full*. Luckily for me, I'm a Nashville native and could commute to campus.

After surviving first semester, I moved on campus and realized that college wasn't just a place to have freedom and friends. It was a place to be accountable for my academic success. This was challenging as I struggled to balance campus and classroom life. Struggling with my courses landed me on academic probation by my sophomore year. Since I wasn't enrolled in school,

I decided to work a full-time job. I continued to visit the campus and attend campus events whenever I could. Not being enrolled in classes didn't seem like the end of the world—until the day I was faced with the ultimate self-reflecting moment.

Standing in the Student Center, I was embarrassingly called a "local" by one of my peers. This didn't sit well with me. A "local" is anyone from Nashville who is not enrolled in college but hangs out on campus. To add insult to injury, it was on the most popular day of the week:

a Wednesday. If you've ever been to TSU, on a Wednesday, anybody who's anybody is going to be in the Student Center. It was in that moment that I realized I had to get back in good academic standing.

My junior year had to be the most pivotal point for me. This time, I didn't have academic issues. But I was a victim of a fatal gunshot to the face that almost took my life the day after Thanksgiving. This situation showed me the camaraderie of my HBCU, TSU. While in the hospital for three days, my college peers filled the hospital room, lobby and waiting rooms daily to check on my wellbeing. Due to my injury, and being so close to exam time, I was not able to finish my semester *in the classroom*. Rallying around me, my peers contacted my professors, obtained my homework assignments and brought them to my home so I could complete the semester. The TSU administration arranged for me to take necessary exams upon my return that upcoming spring semester. *They* did not fail me. This was truly a blessing! I was back on track.

Upon returning to school, I changed my major to the Business Information System (BIS) program, which was new to TSU at that time. Being in the BIS program relocated me from the main campus to the Avon Williams Campus (AWC). Big change. Big impact. While on the AWC, I was introduced to Dr. David King, a new professor who was teaching my networking class. Our relationship was unique. He recognized that I wasn't truly retaining the material from his class. Thoughtfully enough, he provided me with hands-on experience, successfully teaching me computer skills. Dr. King taking interest in me and going the extra mile to ensure I was prepared was another example of the positive impact that TSU has made on my life. He always laughed and told me, "Juan, you may be learning computers in my class today, but you're going to run your own business one day. It may not be computers, but it will be something great."

That entire semester developed into Dr. King teaching me life skills: about being a man, being an adult, being responsible, and to never let anyone control my destiny. His influence and inspiration encouraged me to focus even more on my academics and my future. When I finished my upper classes, I was a totally different student and a different person from when I first enrolled at TSU. The values instilled in me from my HBCU experience plays a major part in who I am today.

Never would I have imagined that a child from Nashville, with no intentions of higher education, would gain so much from an HBCU. Never would I have imagined that a child from Nashville, who had the will and drive to be successful in life, yet little direction, would gain so much from an HBCU. The common theme I relate to today is, "Never give up and always push through. Don't let unopened doors remain closed. Keep knocking or find another door." Based on the trials and hurdles I experienced while trying to obtain my bachelor's degree, I could have found any excuse to give up. But every time I wanted to quit, I found a way to jump the hurdle and continue the race. This mentality has taught me perseverance. It had shaped my success today—in my life, career and through my community involvement.

I'm currently an owner of "The Shower Pros" company, which is one of the most prestigious remodeling companies in Middle Tennessee. I'm the director of a 501(c) (3) non-profit known as the Nashville Youth Basketball Association (NYBA), which is the largest youth basketball program in Tennessee. We operate basketball programs year-round through leagues, camps, tournaments and national basketball events. NYBA allows me to give back to my fellow TSU alumni as a coach and mentor to their children. I'm also the executive director for the

Forever Don Foundation, which is a non-profit branch of the NYBA program. It focuses on saving youth through activities and programs to increase their awareness of violence, while surrounding them with positive men and women mentors. I founded and own the Forever Don Brand, which specializes in the creation of tee shirts, joggers, hoodies and various athletic apparel. I also serve as the youth director for Evans Hill Missionary Baptist Church in Nashville.

My biggest success, and ultimate win from attending TSU, was meeting my wife, Diamond. As alumni, we both devote our time to assisting and supporting our alma mater. We are products of an HBCU, and our daughter is the product of an HBCU experience!

Proverbs 16:9 says, *A man's heart plans his way, but the Lord directs his steps.*

About Juan Adams

Juan Adams, was born and raised in Nashville, TN where he pursued his college career at Tennessee State University receiving his B.S. degree in Business Information Systems. Post TSU he started three ventures. First, Extended Services, LLC, a home remodeling company based out of Middle, TN now known as "The Shower Pros". Secondly, "The Forever Don Foundation" a nonprofit was birthed to honor his 18-year-old son that lost his life to senseless gun violence in the Nashville community. This foundation had such a positive impact on Middle TN youth, that it expanded to his third business venture known as "Forever Don Brand". The brand consists of urban clothing and sports gear. He also works for the Nashville Youth Basketball Association, a local non-profit where he serves as Asst. Director, while coaching local and national teams. His love for Christ positioned him at Evans Hill church as the youth director. His greatest accomplishment is being a husband, father, and giving back to his community.

KEINETHA POWERS

Love Jones
KeiNetha Powers

Attending a Historically Black College or University (HBCU) is an experience like no other. The sense of community is undeniable and the genuine care for students is apparent. But when I stepped foot on the campus of Tennessee State University (TSU), I had no idea just how much my alma mater would mean to me in my adult life. Experiencing the implicit attitude of black excellence, as well as building the lifelong relationships with my peers, has proven to be beneficial in my life. I wouldn't trade it for anything in this world. It's amazing to think I would have missed out on all the glorious memories and experiences had my parents not demanded that I attend TSU. I greatly appreciate their firmness in hindsight; however, at the time, I was determined to not attend TSU by any means necessary.

My parents always had the explicit expectation that I would attend college. I agreed with them, but I always contended that *where* I would attend school was up for grabs. HBCUs are a tradition in my family. My parents attended and met each other at the University of Arkansas in Pine Bluff (UAPB). I always looked forward to attending homecoming with them. I was infatuated with the majorettes. The way their long legs so effortlessly kicked toward the heavens, all while keeping with the beat of booming bass drums, mesmerized me. The energy among the alumni was electric. It was so much fun to see my parents laugh and enjoy themselves with their college friends. However, that's all it ever was for me: fun. I attended a predominantly white high school and erroneously believed that my college experience would likely be more of the same. Surely, attending an HBCU couldn't afford me the opportunities of rigorous academic challenge, while simultaneously give a roaring good time. I didn't know that was possible. It never crossed my mind that I would attend an HBCU.

During the summer before my senior year of high school, my parents had a serious sit-down with me. My dad did most of the talking and *told* me I was going to Tennessee State University, without room for discussion. My dad noted that, since my older brother Marcus was in his junior year there, he could "keep watch" over me. Of course, in hearing such a statement, I instantly became as prickly as a porcupine.

"I don't need nobody to keep watch over me! I'm an adult!" I hissed. To my defense, I was a responsible teen. I worked two jobs while in high school, was a member of the dance team, and held a 3.5 grade point average. I had all of this under control. I believed my parents were experiencing a serious lapse of early empty-nesters syndrome and had lost their minds. Nonetheless, no matter how much I pleaded, argued or pouted with my parents, they were firm on their decision. There was no use. My dreams were dashed, and I was devastated.

I was utterly determined *not to* attend TSU. So, I did what any cunning, know-it-all, strong-willed teenager would do to rebel against their parents' wishes. I started scheming and devised a plan to conveniently "forget" about the application deadline to apply to TSU. I was sure to meet all of the other university application deadlines, however. Much to my chagrin, my dad royally foiled my plans. He knew me all too well. He requested all of the admissions information directly from the school and scheduled a campus visit. We were slated to meet with admissions representatives to complete and submit the application. Needless to say, I was livid.

Nonetheless, I continued to plot and plan *not to* attend TSU until the final days. I thought my last-ditch effort of being accepted to a prestigious university on the west coast would completely derail my parents' mission. I was awarded a partial scholarship to a predominantly white institution. However, I wasn't concerned with that as much as I wanted to journey as far away from Alabama as possible. However, my parents refused, citing the distance from home, and their lack of financial assistance, as the culprits. So, here I was, wallowing in despair because my efforts were thwarted. I reluctantly accepted the offer to attend TSU and begrudgingly prepared to relocate to Nashville, Tennessee late in the summer of 2002.

When I arrived at TSU, I had conflicting emotions. I was excited to start my life as a college student, but I was lowkey resentful that I was at the very university I tried so hard not to attend. To further complicate this journey, my high school boyfriend (and now husband) was also starting his freshman year at TSU. To say there was a lot riding on this major transition was an understatement.

Marcus, my older brother, took me under his wing and introduced me to the key staff and faculty members. According to him, he was "a big deal" because of his connections after having had several work-study positions in various departments on campus. He was able to finesse my housing assignment and configure my schedule. He even asked his fraternity brothers to move me into my dorm. This was great and all, but I was still stuck in my feelings. I wasn't happy. I cried at least twice a day during my first week on campus. I was angry at my parents, annoyed that my plans were spoiled. I was ready to pack it up and go back to Alabama.

My entire mood and perspective shifted after I was accepted into the University Honors Program at TSU. The director of the program at the time, Dr. Sandra Holt, invited me to an office meeting to discuss changing my schedule to accommodate honors courses. Maybe it was her motherly disposition, or possibly her passion for students, that caused me to feel safe in her office. Whatever it was, I began to weep in her office after she asked, "How are you liking TSU?" She could visibly see my hurt and disappointment. I told her of my scheme to *not* attend TSU and all the complex and conflicting emotions I was having. She quietly came over to me and allowed me to cry in her arms.

She softly wiped my tears and told me, "Baby, your parents knew you needed community and care. You can't get that at just any ole university."

I knew deep down she was nothing but right. She talked of the spirit of "Big Blue Country" and the expectation of excellence of all students. Dr. Holt mentioned how brilliance was literally everywhere, if I would only open my eyes to see it. She explained how the honors program provided amazing opportunities for professional development. No other place could groom me for the real world like TSU would. From that day forward, I saw the university and myself differently. I could feel the buzzing energy and excitement on Wednesdays in the student center. I loved the sense of pride I felt when I gleefully sang, "I'm so glad I go to TSU!" I understood that a PWI could never offer the spirit of thriving merit that TSU so graciously offered to me. All the diabolical scheming was over, and I was now charged to step into greatness.

The life-changing incident with Dr. Holt, along with other childhood experiences, spurred me to direct my educational path to the field of psychology. I wanted to help others sort through challenging emotions in order to live their lives authentically. I wanted to hold space for those that, like me, were struggling to find their way. Because of that genuine outpour of love and concern for me, I have grown into a career as a licensed psychotherapist in Atlanta.

I had once-in-a-lifetime adventures with friends. I joined the incomparable Greek organization, Alpha Kappa Alpha Sorority, Inc. I developed long-lasting friendships and priceless connections. If it wasn't for my time at TSU, I wouldn't have been so well prepared and confident in my abilities to seek further education as I entered the real world.

My four years at Tennessee State University were some of the best years of my life. I grew into my true self while I was there. I learned how to navigate the ever-present pressures of being a black woman in an unappreciative world. I challenged myself to go above and beyond in order to embody the *"Think. Work. Serve."* motto of Tennessee State University. And while I intentionally attempted to scheme and wreck the divinely orchestrated plans of my attendance, Tennessee State University gave me more than I could have possibly ever dreamed.

About KeiNetha Powers

K. Mia Powers is a Psychotherapist with more than a decade of experience in the mental health field. She obtained a bachelor's degree in Psychology from Tennessee State University and a Master's degree in Human Development Counseling from Vanderbilt University as well as an additional Master's degree in Clinical Psychology from the Georgia School of Professional Psychology.

Mia's work experience with children has spanned several areas; including teaching language acquisition to children diagnosed with Autism Spectrum disorders, assisting students and families during the special education eligibility process, as well as facilitated the healing journey of children affected by severe mental illness. In addition, she has supported the healing process of refugees and immigrants impacted by experienced torture and violence in their native countries. Currently, Mia is a Psychotherapist at T2S Enterprises where she works collaboratively with individuals to build life balance, shift perspectives, examine relationships, and recover from previous traumas.

When she is not providing therapy services, Mia enjoys spending time with her husband, 7 year-old daughter, and 4 year-old son. She also enjoys traveling, yoga, and writing.

DWAYNE WOODS

The Wood
Dwayne Woods

Honestly, I never thought I would be where I am today. I have to reflect on how instrumental attending Tennessee State University (TSU) has been on my life. Growing up in Hollywood, North Memphis, Tennessee, and living in a low-income household, my community glorified sports, violence and drugs. The only things I knew about was going to school, playing sports and not getting into trouble. A lot of my peers played basketball; therefore, I gained a love for basketball, as well. I played basketball throughout high school, but I didn't have a plan of action for what I would do with my life once I graduated high school. I had a few jobs while in high school, but again, I never thought about life *after* high school. Until my friend, DeAnn, told me she submitted a college application on my behalf to Tennessee State University, I didn't have a clue what I would do next.

Initially, I was shocked. I immediately felt like I didn't meet the requirements to get into college; however, all that changed when I received my acceptance letter to attend Tennessee State University. Up to that point, I only knew that HBCU stood for a "historically black college or university." My mother attended LeMoyne-Owen College and became a member of Alpha Kappa Alpha Sorority, Inc. However, she didn't show me what being a part of an HBCU would consist of. So, there I was, preparing to go to college, with no clue of what to expect. Not to mention, I didn't have the finances to buy what I needed for college. Unbeknownst to me, I didn't know TSU would teach me lifelong lessons about friendships, entrepreneurship, corporate America and philanthropy. I didn't know TSU would provide me with an endless bond with people I have no blood relation to.

Once I arrived on campus, I felt alone and completely out of my "comfort zone." I had to take development classes, which made me feel less deserving. I didn't feel worthy of being there. But, once I crossed paths with the late Dr. Lois Harlston, she quickly changed my whole perspective about college. Dr. Harlston became my favorite teacher. She recognized my

107

struggles with her classes and took the extra time to ensure that I performed well in her class. Not only did her care and concern apply to her class, but it applied to the rest of my life. She wrote many recommendation letters for me to join on-campus organizations. We also shared insights on Greek life due to my mother also being a member of Alpha Kappa Alpha Sorority, Inc. such as herself.

I wouldn't consider myself a "social butterfly," but I am socially active. As a result, I've built strong friendships and relationships with many people on campus. During my freshman year, I met a few guys on the basketball courts, which later grew into a brotherhood that we share to this day. Four gentlemen and I would literally do everything together—sports, parties, homework, traveling and countless other things. We referred to our crew name as "PSP08," which was known for cracking endless amount of jokes with each other and at others for fun (people from Memphis would reference this as "checking.")

We enjoyed each other's company to the point we spent nearly every day together. We watched each other literally grow from boys to men like the movie, *The Wood*. Since college, we have done so much together and grown in so many aspects. We have supported each through the best and worst times, through business ventures, from funerals to weddings. Over the years, I was blessed with the opportunity to be a groomsman in three of their weddings and became an uncle to six beautiful children. Once I start a family of my own, they will be instrumental in my family's lives as well.

Over the years, I developed brotherhoods through various organizations on campus.

I joined organizations such as Generation of Educated Men (GEM), the NAACP and Alpha Kappa Psi Business Fraternity, Incorporated. My involvement with these organizations became the foundation for building friendships that ultimately led to unwavering, lifelong relationships and friendships. TSU inspired me and I felt like I was a part of a family, outside of my blood family.

I soon learned about the many TSU traditions that would ultimately kick off the school year. Courtyard Wednesdays, Fish Fridays in the Café, the Student Center, Kean Hall, the John A. Merritt Classic, the Southern Heritage Classic and the Atlanta Football Classic. Then, after the classics were over, it was time to gear up for homecoming. It was at homecoming where I understood, learned and valued the HBCU culture more. I learned about many Greek organizations and how influential each organization was on campus, especially Kappa Alpha Psi Fraternity, Inc.

While finally feeling a part of the TSU family, I was placed on financial aid probation. If I could not pay out of pocket, I would have to drop out. I definitely did not want that. Being the oldest of eight children, I made it my purpose to be the example for my siblings and family.

I wanted to show them that education is important, as well as embracing the HBCU culture—specifically TSU. TSU is a family. Due to the financial aid staff and administration believing in me, I received just enough financial aid to graduate.

After graduating in 2010, I realized that those relationships and friendships I developed in undergrad still applied to my life. It was in that moment that I realized the perks of being a graduate of TSU. I joined Hendersonville Alumni Chapter of Kappa Alpha Psi Fraternity, Inc., which was mostly composed of TSU graduates. My fraternity brothers and their families taught me that the TSU family has no bounds. TSU and the Kappas assisted in giving me jobs and places to stay. They introduced me to travelling and pushed me into entrepreneurship (Uncharted Horizons Marketing, LLC).

Immediate support from the TSU family led Uncharted Horizons Marketing, LLC to produce several regional, and one international, website of the year awards. I started a fitness challenge and foundation called The Ms. Lucille Challenge (MLC), which focuses on 87 consecutive days of fitness in remembrance of my grandmother, the late Lucille Bernard. With the overflowing support from the TSU family, the challenge and foundation grew enormously. Even when I moved to Houston in January of 2019, my TSU family was there to help me get acclimated to the city. I was so overwhelmed by the amount of love and support that I joined the TSU Houston Alumni Chapter.

Attending Tennessee State University was one of the best decisions, if not *the best decision*, of my life. TSU helped mold my way of thinking about life and black communities in general. Attending an HBCU is truly a priceless experience that I do not take for granted.

TSU took a young lost boy from the hood and shaped me into a hard-working employee, entrepreneur and philanthropist.

About Dwayne Woods

Dwayne Woods, Co- Founder & CEO of Unchartered Horizons Marketing, LLC and Owner of the Ms. Lucille Challenge Foundation is a native is Memphis, TN. He attended Tennessee State University where is received his bachelor's degree in Business Administration with a concertation in marketing. Shortly after receiving his bachelor's degree, Dwayne returned to school and received his Master of Business Administration at Argosy University. A proud member of Kappa Alpha Psi Fraternity Inc., Dwayne is a very active member. Due to Dwayne's commitment to his local chapter, they hired to his company to build their website. Since building the chapter's website, the chapter has been awarded several regional website of the year awards and one international website of the year award. In 2017, Dwayne relocated to Memphis to become a caregiver for his late grandparents. During his time in Memphis, he launched the Ms. Lucille Challenge Foundation which combined his passion for fitness and serving the community. Dwayne relocated to Houston, TX in 2019, where he works as a Sr. Business Analyst at Fortune 50 company and continues to grow his business and foundation.

MERIDITH MILLER RUCKER

Brown Sugar
Meridith Miller Rucker

I remember being sweaty. The heat of August in Tennessee carries the strength of 1,000 suns. I still wore bootcut jeans and a denim halter to freshman orientation. It was the summer of 2001. I'd made it to the last orientation before the academic year began at Tennessee State University. A few months prior, I paid a $360 deposit to hold my spot at Spelman. Back then, the Atlanta University Center was the holy grail of the Historically Black College and University (HBCU) experience. I had been claiming Spelman since I was 16 years old. But somewhere inside, another path was calling. I remember dialing Spelman's business office and asking for a refund.

"You sure?" the woman on the other line questioned.

I was. At the time, it seemed like a simple pivot. But I couldn't have predicted the remarkable impact that change in course would have on my life's trajectory. Walking around in head-to-toe denim at orientation covered in perspiration felt like a rite of passage. My hair was frizzy, and my clothes were damp. But my excitement was unmatched. I was on course.

I remember when I first fell in love with hip hop. It was somewhere between Luke's

I Wanna Rock and Dr. Dre's *Nothing But a G Thang* of 1992, and The Notorious B.I.G.'s 1994 release of *Ready to Die.* I'm sure community pools, freeze cups, favorite cousins and cute boys were involved. I *don't* remember when I fell in love with TSU. I wanted to go *away*, away. No school that was two hours and 45 minutes up Interstate 40 seemed worldly enough. I had stars in my eyes. I wanted to "go places" and "see things." But my respect for TSU flourished when I attended the Southern Heritage Classic. Memphians rooted for the home team and I loved every minute of it.

There was magic in that crisp, fall air that tousled my curls, danced across my cheeks, and always coaxed a Cheshire grin from my lips. It raced through the raised hands of fans in stadium seats and swirled around the hips of the Sophisticated Ladies sashaying through the stands. That same air erupted in loud claps from the high-fives of old friends and melted over new acquaintances hugging for the first time. The sights and sounds, as well as the bright lights in Liberty Bowl Stadium, shined on a sea of smiling black faces and the low hum from a million little conversations. Blue and white pom poms waving, the clear, robust sound of the Aristocrat of Bands beaming while the red, silky lining of their capes courted the crowd like a matador to a bull. In the parking lot, portable radios and speakers battled each other, blasting everything from Lil John and the Eastside Boys, to Earth, Wind & Fire. I remember the scents from grills, deep fryers and smokers that signaled we were in the midst of a family affair. All the elements together created the kind of vibe you wanted to inhale and roll around in your spirit. After a few years of breathing that energy, TSU was in my cypher.

My parents were surprised when I added TSU to my college list. I was extremely studious (*a proud nerd*) and TSU's "party school" reputation was well-established. My best friend and I scheduled our first visit. Her mom took us to the admissions office where we met a recruiter who had a winning mix of coolness and familiarity, which made him feel like my favorite, older cousin.

"Imma take them on a tour now, Mama," he said, walking us toward the courtyard. "They gon' be fine. I promise."

We walked around for 20 minutes. That same vibe I'd grown to love at the Classic was on the campus. The same magic was in the air. I don't remember what we saw or who we talked to on that tour. But I never forgot how I *felt*. I felt like I was *home*. The following year when I made that phone call to ditch Spelman and head to the "Land of Golden Sunshine," I knew I was headed in the right direction.

I believe TSU was already written in the cosmos for many of us who journeyed there. Just as stars connect in a vast, violet sky to form constellations—something bigger and greater—so do HBCU students when we connect. My lifelong, life-changing friendships from TSU have been the

114

biggest return on investment from my time at an HBCU. The day my best friend and I moved into Mary Wilson Hall, a cute girl with short hair stuffed under a baseball cap stood in our doorway, holding 20 shopping bags.

"I'm locked out of my room," she said. "Can I sit with you guys?"

"Sure!" we exclaimed in unison. We talked with her for hours. I felt like I'd known her for years. I soon discovered that this was a common experience when meeting fellow Tigers. Many of us were kindred souls, in a sense. Four years later, that girl who knocked on my door pledged Alpha Kappa Alpha Sorority, Inc. with me. Six years after we crossed, she was in my wedding. A year after that, I was in hers. It's been 19 years since the day we met, and we still speak several times a week.

I made similar connections through my campus involvements. I attribute who I am today to the leadership development and personal guidance I got from upperclassmen student government association (SGA) colleagues, and the countless all-nighters I spent in the newsroom with TSU *Meter* staff forged lifelong friendships. One of my fellow editors was a bridesmaid in my wedding, and I'll be in hers this fall. Another fellow editor and close friend married that best friend who I was supposed to room with at Spelman. Our love for each other, like the connections we all made, never faded.

The light that we carry that drew us all to this place hasn't faded, either. When you see us together at homecomings, weddings, conferences or bottomless mimosa brunches, we give off supernova energy. But we are all major in our own right. TSU was our training ground. That magic air was the wind beneath our wings that propelled us to our wildest dreams. TSU wasn't as far away from home as I wanted to be, but it allowed me to experience the diversity of the whole world on one campus through various languages, cultures, religions and ideologies. My growth and development there as a communications major and Spanish minor led me to study overseas in Europe. I went on to earn a graduate degree in magazine journalism from New York University. We've all had amazing, impactful careers because of TSU, and our stories are still being written.

Though we travel different roads to our HBCUs, I like to think that black stars (hint: that's all of us) aligning with HBCUs are like partners aligning in a marriage. Sometimes, it's arranged, such as children of legacies choosing to attend the institutions of their parents. Like some lovers, maybe you never imagined choosing your HBCU, but forces of nature drew you together. In every union of a black star to an HBCU, each partner brings something to the table. You help each other grow. You celebrate wins and weather through the losses. Through accountability and support, you work to help each other bloom into the best versions of yourselves. These sacred unions withstand the test of time.

When I was choosing a college, my mother said, "There are hundreds of HBCUs in this country. Pick one." Both of my parents are products of HBCUs. My mother later became the first woman president of her alma mater. We champion HBCUs for affording black students the opportunities and an educational environment that they may not get at a predominantly white institution. Historically, this looked like our people not having *the right* to be educated with white students because of slavery and Jim Crow laws. Today, this looks like an educational system that sometimes fails students of color, making it difficult for them to compete at predominantly white institutions. But the statistics remain crystal clear: Black students who attend HBCUs fare better academically, socially and professionally than their counterparts who attend predominantly white institutions. Those statistics are evident in me and my fellow HBCU brothers and sisters.

I don't remember getting that $360 back. But it was a small price to pay for this star-filled journey that I continue to travel with my Tiger family through our TSU roots. If you're ever in Tennessee, or anywhere in the world, and a gust of air tickles your senses, or a star winks at you from the night sky, a TSU Tiger might be near. That's our magic. The light that binds and connects each of us honors the light in each and every one of you.

About Meridith Miller Rucker

Meridith Miller Rucker is a writer and programming expert specializing in youth leadership development and social and emotional learning. With over a decade of experience in education and media, she's worked to generate young adult content and create opportunities to increase youth achievement.

Meridith is the Director of Program Development for BRIDGES, a Memphis-based non-profit, where she designs and implements leadership curricula and experiential programming that annually services 6,000 youth. Prior to BRIDGES, she was Director of First and Second Year Programs at LeMoyne-Owen College where she lead the expansion of Freshman Seminar to First Year Experience and increased the College's retention by 15 percent. Her additional education work includes writing policy, facilitating training and creating digital coursework.

Meridith received her bachelor's in communications from Tennessee State University and her master's in magazine journalism from New York University. She has been an editor for *CosmoGIRL!* and *Soap Opera Weekly,* and she led the launch of teen magazine *Pixie,* which became its publisher's highest seller at newsstand. Her work has appeared in *Glamour*, the *New York Post*, *Hallmark* and *Southern Women.*

Meridith enjoys yoga, music, and traveling, and she lives in her hometown of Memphis with her husband Shawn and two sons, Logan and Lenox.

CHRISTOPHER SMITH

The Inkwell
Christopher Smith

I will never forget walking into Kean Hall for that first day of Convocation. As a highly recruited athlete, I had reservations about moving so far from home to Tennessee. That day,

I knew I made the choice that would change my life. The crowd grew quiet as the university president spoke.

"Every morning in Africa, a gazelle wakes up. It knows it must run faster than the fastest lion, or it will be killed. Every morning in Africa, a lion wakes up. It knows it must outrun the slowest gazelle, or it will starve to death. It doesn't matter whether you are a lion or a gazelle. When the sun comes up, you'd better be running."

This powerful African tale is one that many TSU alums know very well. It was the story that inspired the young, impressionable boy from Florida who took his shot and chose to bet on himself when he accepted a scholarship to run track in Tennessee! It feels like it was just yesterday when the crowd grew eerily silent as our president, Dr. James Hefner, echoed those iconic words. It was almost as if we could all sense that this was not a moment we should forget.

These words continue to shape many of us into the people we are today. It was a speech that would be repeated at every major function and event that Dr. Hefner spoke at throughout my maturation at TSU. These words became a mantra. I'm appreciative of the repeated use of this affirmation for students of the HBCU that has become such an important influence in my life.

I once found myself watching a documentary on the hunting habits of the African lion. In the documentary, it mentioned how the lions hunt in groups called *prides*. I was fascinated to find out that it is the female lions that do most of the hunting, as they are faster and more agile than the powerful male lion. The male lion is strong, but slow. When they begin to hunt, the female lions circle behind the gazelles, hidden in the brush. Once they are in place, the male lion lets out his mighty roar, which startles the gazelles. The gazelles instantly run away from the roar, toward the waiting ambush. When I watched that powerful scene, I was immediately reminded of those words bellowed by Dr. Hefner like it was coming from the mighty African lion. But in my older age, I realized that second lesson that laid hidden in plain sight by his words.

Every day, the lion must hunt to eat. But it takes a team to accomplish its goal. It was not about the success of one lion, but the role that the pride played in accomplishing the goal. Our success was not just about the individual success of any of us who heard those words. It was about the legacy that we could leave to inspire others, and how our success could help bring others along, as well.

But there was another powerful narrative that the 18-year-old me missed—the story of the gazelle. At 18, I understood the message to keep running. What I missed was *what happened* when that lion roared. See, sometimes life will roar at you in a way that will shake you to your core. Many of us will be like the gazelle; we will turn to run in the what appears to be the long shot to freedom. But, in all actuality, if we had actually run *toward* the roar, we would have stood a better chance at success and escaping the much slower, less agile male lion!

It was common for Dr. Hefner to end every speech by reminding every student of those who came before us and the success they achieved. Not to brag, but rather for us to understand that we, too, could aspire to greatness. He was not telling us that we should be the *next*

Wilma Rudolph, Dr. Levi Watkins, Congressman Harold Ford, Sr., State Senator Thelma Harper or Oprah Winfrey. Better yet, he wanted to inspire us to be the greatest version of ourselves.

These words encouraged me to try new things. Like many college students, I went through many decisions of what to do with my career. At one point, I wanted to be an aeronautical engineer. Then, I wanted to be a physical therapist. I landed with a degree in political science and have become a National Democratic Strategist.

I have had the privilege to work for presidential candidates such as Senator Hillary Clinton, Senator Bernie Sanders and Senator Amy Klobuchar. I worked for historic congressional races for Congressman Travis Childers of Mississippi and Congressman Sanford Bishop of Georgia. I managed field programs for Senator Harry Reid of Nevada and elected Democratic mayors in red states like Omaha Mayor Jim Suttle, Connie Moran of Ocean Springs, Mississippi, and Parker Wiseman of Starkville, Mississippi.

I am most proud of the skills I developed to work with minority candidates across the country like Congressman Chuy Garcia, Lt. Governor Justin Fairfax, Minority Leader Stacey Abrams and Mayor Andrew Gillum.

I learned everything I know about campaigns from my HBCU, TSU. As we go through life, or in this case, any campaign, sometimes you're the lion. But most times, you're the gazelle. When you're the gazelle, you're faced with challenges that have you start as the underdog. This is not the end of the story, though. It is still up to you to find the strength to run faster than the lion that is out to get you. You must wake up after setbacks, challenges, public scrutiny and when people do not think you have a chance. In my line of work, the gazelle can inspire the world to be a better place. There will always be other gazelles that watch you being chased by the powerful lion. Some will write you off. But when they see you come out on the other side stronger, you will prove that the value of one's desire to thrive can be stronger than just surviving.

Then, there are those times when you are the lion. This is when you have reached the top of your life's safari. You are what others see as the king of the jungle. The lesson Tennessee State University taught me was that, no matter how powerful you become, you must still wake up every morning and hunt! This lesson is hard because this is the lesson of humility. There will be many days when the herd outruns you in life and campaigns. But you still must eat. Others still depend on you. Your success is not just your own. It is about your lion pride. When you are a leader, you can never forget the responsibility that comes along with your position. You must wake up with the same motivation to break barriers and inspire the next lion to be faster and stronger than you.

For years, Tennessee State University has been producing lions and gazelles that have been inspiring their tribes to get up every morning running. It is my affirmation to inspire change in a country that has historically placed obstacles in front of minority and disenfranchised groups. I attest today to those who are watching. Sometimes, I will be the lion and sometimes, I will be the gazelle. But every morning, when the sun comes up, I will wake up running!

Whether you are the lion or the gazelle, remember that someone is always watching you, waiting to be inspired by your accomplishments to become—not the *next you*—but the best version of themselves.

I thank the Flying Tigers, W.U.A.N., Alpha Phi Omega, B.L.A.C.K., The Honors Program, Alpha Theta Chapter of Kappa Alpha Psi Inc., Dr. Sandra Holt, Dr. Bill Hardy, Dr. James Hefner and, most importantly, Tennessee State University for this lesson.

About Christopher Smith

Christopher Smith is a National Democratic Strategist and cast member on Disney+ show Encore. He is sought after by high-profile candidates, nonprofit organizations and elected leaders to provide targeted strategies, progressive oversight and crisis management.

He is president of the Campaign Engineers, Campaign Lessons and Co-Founder of the National Political Consultants and Organizers Association, an organization created to recognize the minority organizers and operatives in the movement and political space.

Mr. Smith has worked on dozens of local, state and national campaigns across all 50 states and US Territories as a manager, senior advisor and general consultant. Recent highlights include serving as deputy campaign manager for Stacey Abrams for Governor and Senior Advisor for Field Strategy for Andrew Gillum for Governor during the primary. Mr. Smith served as deputy national field director for Vermont Senator Bernie Sanders' Presidential bid, and led Mississippi Democrat Travis Childers to one of the largest upsets in U.S. history, in a congressional region that leaned 14 percent Republican. Other clients have included: U.S. Senators Harry Reid, Mary Landrieu and Kay Hagen; and Congressmen Sanford Bishop

KAREN POLK

Something New
Karen Polk

Born and raised on the southside of Chicago, I've been passionate about learning since the first day that I started school. There was never a doubt in my mind that I would one day attend college and major in accounting. Most of my family, including my mother, attended Jackson State University (JSU). I knew that's where I *did not* want to go! I didn't have anything against JSU, but I knew I didn't want to go there. I had a list of the HBCUs I was interested in.

I narrowed my choices to at least three. Although I had decided to attend Prairie View A&M University (PVAMU), I somehow changed my mind at the last minute. I appreciated PVAMU for returning my housing deposit. When I told people that I was going to Tennessee State University (TSU), they said something in relation to me going to the school "that Oprah attended." Attending TSU turned out to be one of the best decisions I've ever made.

I started my freshman year in August of 2001. I heard the terms, "TSU!" "Tigers!" and "Big Blue Country" from the moment I stepped on campus. Staff and students were very welcoming and helpful as I moved way too many of my belongings into my small dorm room on the fifth floor of Wilson Hall. I was assigned a "triple" room, which meant I had to share my room with two other people. I grew up as an only child. Needless to say, it took me a while to adjust to dorm life. Luckily for me, one of my roommates was hardly ever in the room. When she was there, she made sure I had food! The dorm director and resident assistants made sure we settled in fine.

One time, all the girls in the dorm were surprised with care packages that included candy and a stuffed animal from their family and friends. Prior to that evening, the dorm director and/or resident assistants mailed an order form to our parents and provided them with details about what they were planning to do. I couldn't believe that my mom didn't tell me, but I was so excited to get something! It took a while to adjust to my new environment,

125

but I finally got acclimated. To this day, I'm not sure how I always made it on time to class from one side of campus to the opposite side of campus. Maybe it's because people from Chicago walk fast (Kanye shrug).

Prior to attending college, I really didn't care much for football games. That was before I experienced the TSU Aristocrat of Bands half-time performance during the John A. Merritt Classic. For days, I thought about not going. Friday rolled around, and I had nothing planned for Saturday. I decided to get a ticket on Friday since everyone else was talking about going to the game. I figured I should go if I didn't want to be the only person stuck on campus. Little did I know that a football game would be so much fun. It was totally different from my high school football games, to say the least. I found out that everybody—students and local residents—attended TSU football games. I managed to even travel out of town to some of the other classics, mainly to see and hear the Battle of the Bands against other HBCUs. That was just an introduction to what my homecoming experiences would be like. Homecoming consists of thousands of people and festivities that last a whole week. Even though the fun begins in undergrad, it gets better every year after graduation.

Most people go to college anticipating meeting new friends. I met *family*. Literally and figuratively. I met one of my cousins for the first time one afternoon in calculus class. If it wasn't for the teacher taking attendance, who knows if we would have ever met. I knew we were both attending TSU at the same time because one of my aunt's mentioned it to me. But I didn't have a lot of details or contact information. When I heard the teacher say my last name, but it was preceded by a different first name, I instantly thought, *That must be him.* Rarely do I meet people with the same last name.

We formally met after class. Both of our majors were business-related, so we had some of the same classes over the years. It worked in our favor because we only bought one book for each class and shared the books as needed. We split the cost each semester, which saved our parents money.

I'm most grateful for never having a negative experience in the bursar's office at TSU. Sometimes, the length of the line prior to the first day of classes was intimidating. Any alum can attest that any clerk in the office greeted students at the window by saying, "Social." That was their way of asking for our social security number. They would proceed with the process after they pulled up our student account. I really didn't care how I was greeted. I just wanted to pay my balance to avoid having my classes purged. I am thankful for the partial scholarship I received from the Chicago chapter of TSU Alumni. I didn't know anything about this group until someone told me to go to Goodwill Manor and see if I could get financial assistance. Goodwill Manor was the alumni relations building on campus. I can't recall who I talked to, but he or she pointed me in the right direction. The Chicago chapter provided me with funds all four years at TSU.

As a native of Chicago, I didn't hesitate to join the Chicago Club when I heard about it on campus. It was good to bond with people in Nashville who could relate to Chicago experiences, especially those who were from the southside like me. We even had similar reactions when it snowed (or should I say *barely snowed*) in Tennessee and everything shut down, including the school. Snow never shut anything down in Chicago. I quickly adapted to the new way of handling a snowstorm. I learned to stock up on food and water before it started snowing, as if I was never going step outside again for days or weeks. The Chicago Club even reunited me with a couple of high school peers who graduated a year or two before me. Some of my fondest memories with this group were when we went to a haunted house *every* Halloween and we ate at a restaurant that was budget-friendly for college students, CiCi's Pizza.

Over the course of four years, I met people from different states, joined several organizations, and gained a lifetime of memories and experiences. As a business/accounting student, I took advantage of joining Phi Beta Lambda Business Fraternity and the National Association of Black Accountants (NABA). Both organizations prepared me for life after college from a workforce perspective. They also provided me with the opportunity to participate in multiple community service projects. In 2004, students from colleges and universities all over Tennessee were selected to intern for the State of Tennessee during the summer. I was one of three TSU students selected for the program and I interned in the audit department. After I completed the summer program, I was able to continue my internship throughout the school year. It has been almost sixteen years since that internship ended, and I'm still in contact with four of the attendees.

I graduated from TSU in 2005. I joined the professional chapter of NABA and later became the chapter secretary. In 2012, I earned my master's degree in economics from Middle Tennessee State University. TSU provided me with the education and leadership skills that have allowed me to grow as an individual and as a professional. I still take advantage of learning at TSU. In 2019, TSU partnered with Apple to provide a technology workshop to students and alumni. Through this program, my team and I were able to pitch an application prototype to a non-profit organization. I promote TSU every chance I get and participate in homecoming festivities every year. It has been almost nineteen years since I moved to Nashville to attend TSU, and I have no regrets. I only go back to Chicago to visit.

I'm so glad I went to TSU.

About Karen Polk

Karen Polk was born and raised in Chicago, IL. After graduating from Lindblom High School in 2001, she decided to attend Tennessee State University. In 2005 she received her BA in Accounting. In 2012 she received her MA in Economics from Middle Tennessee State University. In the Fall of 2020, she will begin the MHA program at Lipscomb University.

Karen is an ambivert that enjoys everything from staying at home to watch re-runs of 90s sitcoms such as A Different World to traveling domestically and internationally with friends. Work keeps her busy, but she finds time to volunteer with local organizations. Although she currently resides in TN, Karen visits "home," Chicago, several times a year.

BRANDON FOLEY

Men In Black

Brandon Foley

As early as I can remember, I knew I would attend a Historically Black College or University (HBCU). Choosing the exact one wasn't clear to me until a few months before my high school graduation. Growing up as the youngest of my mother's four sons in Huntsville, Alabama, I was always surrounded by black excellence. Both of my parents are college graduates, and my father is an HBCU alum (Alabama A&M University).

Growing up, I remember going to basketball and football games, frequently and learning about the HBCU culture. Through the encouragement of my mother, I had opportunities to participate in summer programs that were focused on math and engineering at Alabama A&M. My journey to Tennessee State University (TSU) was a path that two of my older brothers traveled before me. They became a light for me. My oldest brother, who is twelve years my senior, began at TSU in the fall of 1992—which is when I started first grade. He had a scholarship to play in the Aristocrat of Bands. So, at six years old, I experienced the amazing energy of HBCU football games.

My brother, who is four years older than me, decided to follow our oldest brother's footsteps. He enrolled at TSU in the fall of 2000. Oftentimes, he'd come home and tell me how exciting the Student Center/Courtyard was on Wednesdays. He told me that you needed to dress to impress because, "At TSU, the people bring it. You don't need to be seen near the Student Center if you aren't fly!" Hearing about his experiences put TSU at the forefront of colleges when I was deciding which HBCU to attend.

I applied and was accepted to TSU. After graduating from high school in May of 2004,

I set my eyes on Nashville. I completely fell in love with TSU at the mandatory summer orientation for all freshmen students. Seeing students from all over the country come to this university, who were extremely excited about furthering their educational endeavors, was pure love for me! It felt like one big happy family! So much so, I didn't really want to go back to Huntsville for the remaining few weeks of summer break.

Some of my most exciting times in undergrad were during football season. The Atlanta Classic, Tennessee State versus Florida A&M, goes down as one of the best HBCU Classics. The game was always on the last weekend in September, which usually happened to be my birthday weekend. I attended this Classic before I even started attending TSU. My memories in the Georgia Dome, and all the fun had during the Atlanta Classic weekend, are endless. Even when I was in middle school and high school, my mother would check me out of school early to travel from Huntsville to Atlanta to celebrate my birthday and to cheer TSU on to victory over FAMU. My blood runs TSU Blue!

TSU taught me a lot of life lessons—one being that your network determines your net worth. As a junior who was majoring in business, one of the directors in the College of Business advised me about a full scholarship at TSU. Ms. Lisa Smith told me that there was a full scholarship that was created by a late TSU alum and his wife, Dr. Damon and Rachel Lee, for business students that were from either Alabama or California. She encouraged me to apply, and without hesitation, I filled out the necessary documents. After being interviewed for the scholarship, I was awarded a full ride for my last two years at TSU.

My junior year at TSU proved to be a pretty pivotal point in my life. I was awarded a full scholarship, but I also knew that I needed to obtain an internship to gain work experience. My mother constantly told me to make sure that I had an internship before I graduated. When time permitted, I stopped by the Career Development Center to see what opportunities were available.

The director, Dr. Gittens, told me that the Central Intelligence Agency (CIA) was hiring, but I had to have a 3.0 GPA or above. I met the GPA qualifications and sent him my resume. Within a few weeks, I received a phone call from the CIA. After the phone interview, the CIA flew me to

Washington, D.C. to undergo the medical, psychological and polygraph exams. After successfully passing the required exams, as well as the extensive background investigation, I was granted my Top-Secret security clearance. I started as a CIA intern in June of 2007. Prior to starting the internship, a TSU alum reached out to me to let me know she worked for the CIA as well. To my surprise, she was the point of contact who had received my resume from the director of Career Services. This TSU alum played an instrumental part in getting me hired. This experience showed me that TSU connections are all around and we look out for each other!

Because of my amazing experiences at TSU, I am forever indebted to the university that provided me a quality education and showed me so much love. From obtaining a full scholarship to receiving an internship with the CIA, which has now evolved into a 13-year career, I am forever grateful. In 2016, the year that I turned 30, I decided that since a TSU alum was kind enough to start a scholarship that I was a recipient of, I wanted to do the same. God has blessed me, so I want to bless someone else! I talked to my two older brothers, who are both TSU alums, and my mother about my idea. We have officially created the "Collier/Foley Brother's Keeper Scholarship" for students in the College of Business from our hometown.

As things have come full circle regarding my experiences at TSU, I now have a scholarship at the university. I am also currently the CIA's southeast regional recruiter. This position affords me the opportunity to go back to TSU and share opportunities regarding internships and full-time careers with students who may have never considered the CIA as a place of employment. I firmly believe that students are more motivated and encouraged when they see representatives from TSU in positions of influence.

To continuously attract the best and brightest to TSU, I passionately serve as the recruitment chairperson for the alumni chapter in the Washington, D.C. area. I not only want to see my illustrious institution of higher learning succeeding in all aspects, but I want to see it fully thriving as the university of choice for anyone who wants to experience the power of that Big Blue Love! As we say in our TSU-Washington, D.C. alumni chapter, "All HBCUs are good. Some may even be great. But Tennessee State University is world-class!" Tennessee State University will forever be near and dear to my heart! Go Big Blue!

About Brandon Foley

Brandon Foley, a native of Huntsville, Alabama is a proud graduate of Tennessee State University (TSU) where he received his Bachelor's degree in Business Administration with honors in 2008. Prior to graduating from TSU, Brandon accepted an opportunity to intern with the Central Intelligence Agency (CIA) during the summer of 2007 in the Washington, DC area. Brandon is currently the Southeast Regional Recruiter for the CIA where he corporately represents the Agency in Georgia, North Carolina, South Carolina, and Tennessee.

Brandon is a lifetime member of the Tennessee State University National Alumni Association and has served as the Recruitment Chairperson for the Washington, DC Alumni Chapter for the past 10 years. Because of his love and commitment to TSU, Brandon, along with his mother and two of his brothers (also fellow alums), established a scholarship at TSU for students from Huntsville. Brandon has served as a mentor in the College Bound, Inc. mentoring program in Washington, DC and has also tutored with the Education ministry at his church in the DC area.

DR. MALIA R. JACKSON

Lean on Me

Dr. Malia R. Jackson

Strong, prominent, prestigious and nurturing are just a few of the many characteristics to describe the women in my family. When I was growing up, I listened to some of the women in my family talk about their college experiences while attending a Historically Black College and University (HBCU). I enjoyed listening to their stories so much that I was inspired and wanted to attend an HBCU, as well.

After applying to a couple of different colleges and not getting accepted, I became a little discouraged. That all changed just a few weeks later. Sadness turned into joy. I remember receiving my acceptance letter to Tennessee State University like it was yesterday. Someone asked me, "Why do you want to go there?"

"Because my mother went there, and I don't think I would do good if I went anywhere else," I replied. Little did I know that by attending an HBCU, many doors would open for me in the future.

The first set of doors that opened for me were those doors located in Kean Hall during freshman orientation. My father and I walked through those doors, entered Kean Hall, and sat in the front row to listen to the university president, the late Dr. James A. Hefner speak to the incoming freshman class. The takeaway message that I received from that day was, "Always keep good, positive working relationships with your professors because you never know when you will need them." Prior to attending freshman orientation, I was introduced to Dr. Hefner through family connections, which set the tone for building good, positive working relationships. Building good, positive working relationships are important because you never know where those relationships can lead you and what they can do for you. That introduction meant so much to me coming from out-of-state because I was able to attend TSU on a small scholarship.

Another positive influence at TSU was Dr. Michael Ivy in the biology department. Dr. Ivy was always available and has been extremely helpful throughout my collegiate and professional journeys. Keeping good, positive working relationships with professors did not present itself as a challenge while attending TSU because of how supportive the "Big Blue" community was to the students. Although the campus seemed so big at the time, it was home away from home. It was like one, big happy family. The campus was filled with students from various locations with similar backgrounds and cultural experiences. Attending an HBCU allowed me to form lifelong, meaningful friendships.

The second set of doors that opened for me while attending TSU was the charter bus that transported me and my close friends to church every Sunday. My close friend at the time said, "There's a church that has a bus that will pick us up on Sundays. I heard they have good food, and they feed students home-cooked meals." During that conversation with my friend, all I heard was, "...bus that will pick us up on Sundays, good food, students and home-cooked meals." I instantly became a member of this church after I heard the words, "...bus, food, and home-cooked meals." Being away from home, I missed my mother's cooking and I was looking forward to having a good meal.

I went to this church to get fed physically, not knowing that I would also be fed spiritually. The church that I am referring to is Mount Zion Baptist Church where Bishop Joseph W. Walker, III is the lead pastor. Attending an HBCU such as TSU allowed me to find a church home, away from home. It was a church home where I was able to become active in the college ministry and grow spiritually, and I'm still a member today.

Throughout my collegiate tenure at TSU, I met so many influential people, some of which I consider mentors. My late grandmother, who was also a retired educator and a member of Alpha Kappa Alpha Sorority, Inc., served as a spiritual mentor throughout my life. She, too, had a great influence in my life. She inspired me and was the reason why I wanted to become a member of Alpha Kappa Alpha Sorority, Inc. Attending an HBCU allowed me to become a member of the Awesomely Sophisticated Alpha Psi Chapter of Alpha Kappa Alpha Sorority, Inc.

The third set of doors that opened for me while attending TSU were the doors located in the TSU Gentry Complex. I walked through those doors during my senior year in 2007, wearing a cap and gown. Attending an HBCU allowed me to be the first amongst my siblings to graduate from a four-year accredited college and university. I graduated from the College of Health Sciences program with a Bachelor of Science in health sciences, with a concentration in therapeutic studies. Walking out of those doors on that day were both exciting and scary. I was glad to be done with school; yet, I was scared because I was leaving my "Big Blue" family.

Although I had walked through the doors of the TSU Gentry Complex, this was not the end of my journey. This was truly just the beginning. The positive working relationships that I formed throughout my collegiate journey while attending an HBCU helped me continue to walk through more doors throughout my post-academic journey. The supportive and encouraging environment provided by the educators and staff at TSU inspired me and created a passion in me for teaching.

Walking through the doors of an HBCU such as Tennessee State University created a revolving effect. These revolving doors opened once again and allowed me to return and serve as an assistant professor in the Department of Occupational Therapy.

I hope to be as inspiring to the students who I currently educate, just as my former educators were to me. Attending an HBCU such as TSU extended a helping hand to former students like myself. It is my belief that through the extension of a helping hand, there is a future for a better tomorrow.

About Dr. Malia R. Jackson

Dr. Malia R. Jackson is a registered and licensed Occupational Therapist. She is a Tennessee State University graduate of the COHS, B.S. degree in Health Sciences with a concentration in Therapeutic Studies who obtained a Doctor of Occupational Therapy degree from Belmont University. She has had the pleasure of primarily working in the skilled nursing environment as a fieldwork level II student and an occupational therapist. In this capacity, she provided skilled occupational therapy services to both long-term and short-term residents, supervised occupational therapy assistants, and served as a fieldwork educator to fieldwork level II students.

As a fieldwork educator, she provided occupational therapy students with the opportunity to apply academic knowledge through a hands-on learning experience in delivering occupational therapy services to clients in a skilled nursing setting. Her experience working with fieldwork level II students was very positive and reaffirmed her passion for teaching. Her experience through fieldwork, education, and practice allowed her to gain the skills necessary to thrive in an environment that seeks to prepare tomorrow's health care leaders within the Department of Occupational Therapy at Tennessee State University.

DEDDRICK PERRY

House Party
Deddrick Perry

I love the HBCU community and the Historically Black College experience. I believed that going to an HBCU, especially my TSU, would change my life   long before I arrived on campus. I was convinced! Coming out of high school, I needed a change of scenery and access to a larger network. A *different* network. That's exactly what I got when I touched down August 8, 1999.

Joliet, Illinois is where I grew up. Several of my friends from high school attended TSU with me. There were at least eight of us during my freshman year. I was already an outgoing young man, so the social scene at TSU just made it more enjoyable. I came to college expecting a life-changing experience, not necessarily a turn-key economic opportunity. I focused my attention on building meaningful relationships, intellectual exploration, and talking to as many beautiful women as possible!

On campus, I was a bit of a wild man! I enjoyed the nightlife of Nashville after dark and hung with my friends on campus in the gazebos and the Floyd Payne Campus Center during the day. I stayed in Watson Hall during my freshman year, Hale Hall for sophomore and junior year, and The Kappa House my senior year. Tennessee State just felt natural to me.

Learning how to balance business and pleasure would prove to be key for me. As a business investor and operator, my style is very casual. I often meet people at parties and

fundraisers. Thank goodness for TSU-sponsored nightlife teaching me how to be social and productive!

I was president of my fraternity, Kappa Alpha Psi, Alpha Theta Chapter, on campus.

I was also active with the University Honors Program. I had a paid position, and I was an honor student and mentor to incoming freshman honor students. Many of the students in the program have since gone on to do amazing things.

Campus leadership prepared me mentally and emotionally to deal with a wide variety of personalities. Those opportunities also taught me the value of curating institutions. Having a sense of governance as a young adult made acquiring large institutional business assets like hospitals seem natural.

Thank you to Dr. Sandra Holt for leading and expanding the honors department. That experience, for me, normalized the idea of being able to thrive in an environment of high performers. This is something that has benefitted me in innumerable ways. One of the most important components for me was mentorship. University Honors gave me a chance as a student to help onboard incoming freshman honors students and set them up for success in college and in life. I've never stopped this practice. My current mentee, Kevuntez King, is a high performing senior at Tennessee State. I met him after he made national headlines for his business savvy while he was in high school. Kevuntez has been a paid summer intern for four summers at an international hospital I founded in Mexico. University Honors made me a mentor for life!

My paternal grandmother, Dorothy Perry, attended TSU back in the early 50s. I have at least fifteen relatives and ancestors that are TSU alums and/or administrators. For me, TSU is literally family. It was a great feeling to meet old college acquaintances of some of my oldest relatives and get a glimpse into what their lives were like before I was even thought of. Graduating from TSU was like an interactive history lesson about my own family.

Since graduation, my personal network has grown to include so many wonderful people from around the world. Still, my HBCU family is the dominant presence. Oftentimes, I find myself in situations abroad where I may not speak the language or have many acquaintances outside of business. I can count on my friends and fraternity brothers. I communicate via a network of *hilarious* group chats every single day.

I'm so thankful for the lifetime relationships I've gained from TSU.

About Deddrick Perry

Deddrick Perry is a native of Joliet, IL and 2003 graduate of Tennessee State University. He's a private equity investor and entrepreneur. As a resident of Puerto Rico, Deddrick spends most of the year in the Caribbean. He is the Co-Founder of the CHIPSA Hospital and North Beach Oncology Clinic in Playas de Tijuana Mexico. Deddrick supports charitable missions around the world and enjoys travel and public speaking.

ASHLEIGH TILLMAN

A Thin Line Between Love & Hate

Ashleigh Tillman

I made many memories in "The Land of Golden Sunshine." Yet, my fondest memory comes from my time as Miss Tennessee State University. This experience is etched in my mind as a fond, painful and formative journey. Valuable lessons of my reign still haunt—and heal—me today.

It was my freshman year during new student orientation. The first time I saw her, she wore an impeccable blue satin suit, with silver heels to match each rhinestone button down the front of her suit. Her makeup was perfect and timeless. Her hair moved with such ease that it practically looked painted on her. Her jewelry was bright and ornate. However, the pinnacle of her outfit was the large heiress crown that rested atop her head.

She glided across the room and commanded attention from everyone who was present. Her smile was enchanting; it sparkled just like the embellishments on her pageant sash. I knew right then that I had to become *her*. I had to become *queen*.

With all my southern confidence and naivety, I marched right up to this woman and introduced myself. She must've been accustomed to people coming up to her freely by her reaction. She casually turned around, smiled and introduced herself. She asked me about my major and what I was looking forward to most about the school year.

I boldly replied, "I want to become queen."

She smiled. Again, she looked as if she had heard that statement a lot and had rehearsed a response.

"Well, make sure you are ready," she said.

With that, she walked away, smiling and nodding along the way.

I was convinced that I was ready. The queen herself had given me her blessing, no matter how awkward it had been. *What did I have to prepare for?* Little did I know that being "ready" meant more than preparation, but *positioning.*

Like most freshmen, I got overly involved in extracurricular activities and idolized upperclassmen. I observed everything they did. I watched who they connected with, how they prepared themselves for leadership, and how they carried themselves overall. In doing this, I cemented my love for Big Blue. My school spirit was through the roof. I loved being connected to a powerhouse institution in my home state. We made history. And I would soon be a part of that history.

I also realized that, at TSU, everything was a process. Everyone had to pay dues.

If I wanted to be queen, I needed to follow the pathway and pipeline, and position myself accordingly. I needed to prove myself to be worthy of queen first.

Now, I always had a high level of confidence. But somewhere during my collegiate experience, the "imposter syndrome" kicked in. Yes, I was smart, articulate and cute. But did I carry the archetype of a queen?

Would my cocoa brown skin and (then) skinny frame be the standard of a quintessential queen? I soon compared myself to other royal hopefuls who were clear contenders for the crown. All were more shapely, popular and lighter than me.

Still, I pushed forward and implemented my plan. I successfully won two high profile queen positions during my sophomore and junior years.

Whew! Half of the hard part was over. I'd proven to the campus that I was a quality contender. By my senior year, I joined my beloved sorority, remained active in student government, and even maintained a relationship with a handsome southern gentleman. I felt adequately prepared to campaign for Miss TSU.

Campaigning was brutal and overwhelming. It felt like a week-long battle of popularity and loyalty. By the end of it, I was exhausted. I had never worn so much makeup, or so much blue. I'd never talked to so many people and cried as much as I did that week. It all proved to be worth it, though, because I won! Now, the real work started.

During the summer, prior to my reign, I prepared for the year ahead. After my internship, I spent time planning events, shopping for outfits, and working with the royal court to generate the best year possible. I felt ready. I felt prepared.

I was wrong.

The more visible you become, the more you open yourself up for criticism. Everyone has an opinion about something you've done or said, or not. It's like living in a fishbowl or snow globe. Everything you do is under a microscope.

I constantly thought about how I presented myself to the campus community. Could I truly be the archetype of a queen? A chocolate-kissed, awkwardly shaped, short-haired girl in a satin suit and sash?

Although my friends, sorority sisters and supporters encouraged me, loved on me and always kept me grounded, I felt alone.

There is a considerable amount of pressure associated with student leadership. Likewise, there is a significant amount of pressure associated with being queen.

I felt like I couldn't make a mistake. I couldn't have a day off. I needed to work twice as hard to prove that I belonged. I had to show that I was prepared. No matter how friendly, hardworking or relatable I was, people always compared me to others based on my physical appearance. This destroyed my confidence slowly. I became consumed with being queen instead of being *myself.*

It wasn't until a sudden turn of events in the spring semester that my position as queen was stunted. All my preparation washed away. I no longer had the filter of queen to guide my day-to-day activities. For the last five months of my collegiate career, I needed to become Ashleigh. *Just Ashleigh.*

Like anyone who is battling trauma or radical change, I cut my hair. Yes, I went from a well-manicured pixie cut to a tennis ball big chop. The critics had a field day.

Honestly, cutting my hair and stripping away the pomp and circumstance felt *freeing*.

I was finally able to be *myself*. I could hang out with friends more, frequent Nashville bars, dance the night away at clubs, and eat all the fried foods I could find. I had to spend more time learning about myself.

Ironically, I never addressed the issue. I never aimed to prove my disposition. I just let it happen. I learned to fail gracefully and with resilience. During my last semester, I learned more about myself than I did any year prior.

Many people still come up to me today and express their gratitude for my representation as queen: dark skin, slim shape and a down-to-earth personality.

I thank God for the tough life lessons I experienced at TSU. It prepared me for adulthood. It prepared me for real life. I learned the power of grit and grace. I learned how to fall in love with myself through every flaw. My experience prepared me for a career, marriage and family. Where else would I have had such an experience?

Today, I've learned how to create my own definition of a queen.

I was always prepared, even when I didn't know it. The growing pains I experienced at TSU are some of my fondest memories.

Big Blue made me into an adult and a Tiger for life.

About Ashleigh Tillman

Ashleigh Tillman is a native of Memphis, Tennessee. She is a proud graduate of Tennessee State University (B.S. Communications) and the University of Louisville (M.Ed). Currently, she is a PhD in Educational Management candidate from Hampton University graduating in May 2020. Her research focuses on leadership development for NPHC sorority members. A former higher education professional, Ashleigh currently serves as the Manager of Alumni Impact for Teach for America DC and owns a boutique wedding planning business Nicole Noire Event. She is an active member of Xi Zeta Omega Chapter of Alpha Kappa Alpha Sorority, Incorporated, Junior League of Washington DC, Alfred Street Baptist Church and the Greater Washington Urban League Young Professionals Network. In her spare time, Ashleigh enjoys soulful cooking, bargain shopping and entertaining in her home. She resides in Fort Washington, MD with her husband and lovable dog.

MARCUS JOHNSON

Class Act
Marcus Johnson

As a kid from Nashville, TSU has been a part of my life for as long as I can remember. Some of my best memories as a kid included attending events during TSU's homecoming. I always pictured myself as a student at the university. My experience at *thee* Tennessee State University (TSU) was way more than just an education. My experience was about learning how to build true relationships. The relationships that I built helped me in more ways than one. Since my career as a financial planner is predicated on building relationships with clients, my time at TSU helped to build the foundation.

Upon arriving at TSU, I told myself that I would just go to class and study. I'm so glad that I had a change of heart because, if I had not changed my way of thinking, I would have missed out on the best part of college, which was the lifelong bonds I built. I am so thankful that I was able to learn these skills early on because I believe that relationships are the key to a successful career in any field. I chose to attend an HBCU because I wanted to go to an institution that valued people of color. Being at TSU taught me that it was okay to be a young black man in America. It also gave me a deeper appreciation for the beautiful history of the people before me. Being at TSU taught me to think bigger. Bigger than my circumstances, bigger than my environment or even where I came from.

Those principles that were instilled in me inspired me to take an internship on Wall Street in New York the summer before my senior year of college. From that internship, I landed a job on Wall Street after I graduated, which jump-started my career in the financial industry. My love and passion for finance and economics began to grow during my time in high school. However, during my time at TSU, my love and passion for the financial industry grew tremendously through a program in the economics department where we partnered with the TVA. They allowed us to invest real money in the stock market. From that experience alone, I knew exactly what I wanted to do with my life.

Throughout this program, we were able to take concepts we learned from class and project them in the market. In the course of running the fund, we managed a portfolio of over $500,000 and had a return of over 27%. I was able to leverage this experience which I believe is what helped me to land my job on Wall Street. Along with running the fund at TSU, I also became the president of the Economic and Finance Society. During my tenure, I was able to connect with so many students and build a few programs that they are still using in the department today. One of those programs was a mini career fair that brought some of the executives from the financial industry to Tennessee State University. This allowed students like me the opportunity to engage in one-on-ones with some of the big firms in the financial industry. Although being in the financial industry is something that I am grateful for, and Tennessee State definitely helped cultivate that, Tennessee State also helped me tremendously in another area in my life.

Aside from being a financial planner, I am also a jazz saxophonist. While I was a student at TSU, I had my first solo gig as a musician and that molded me into the musician that I am today. I will never forget Coach Pope giving me a shot to perform on campus for a student fashion show. The event went so well that myself, along with a band that I put together at TSU, began performing at all types of events on campus. Shortly after we started, we transitioned from only performing at campus events to also playing at corporate events for companies such as the American Diabetes Association to galas at Vanderbilt. Being a member of TSU Jazz Band shaped my discipline to studying the craft. In my freshman year, I was so excited about making the jazz band because it was only a few people who were given that opportunity. During this time, I thought I may have had some talent, but it wasn't until I met a lot of the great musicians there who pushed me to continue to elevate.

I spent countless hours in the Performing Arts Center practicing and learning from other students. Those hard-working hours, along with guidance from professors on campus, helped lead me to playing with artists such as Elle Varner, John Legend, Cheryl "Pepsii" Riley and more. In the music industry, I was able to build a connection with people from TSU and they helped with producing my first album entitled, "Passion Speaks Louder." A few of the musicians who played on my album were also TSU alumni, and they have gone on to do some great things as well. When my album debuted, it was in the Top 5 on iTunes and Amazon for jazz and stayed on the charts for six weeks.

When I think about everything that I received from TSU, I have to place an emphasis on embracing all of the wonderful people who attended the school and finding ways to build with them so that we all could win! There are so many individuals I could thank who were involved in making my college journey the best it could be, but for now, I would just like to say, thank you TSU.

Thank you for showing me how to build relationships and how to navigate through this cold world. You will always have a special place in my heart. You taught me so much, and for that, I will forever cherish my HBCU college experience. I am forever grateful that I attended Tennessee State University because of all the life lessons I learned. I'm proud to be an alum of *thee* Tennessee State University, and I look forward to that day when I can tell my future kids all about this great university. Go, Tigers!

About Marcus Johnson

Marcus Johnson is an experienced and knowledgeable financial planner from Nashville, TN who is ready to work with you to enhance you and your family's financial future. Marcus has a degree in Economics and Finance from Tennessee State University, and also holds his Series 7, Series 66, life insurance, and health insurance licenses. After six years working on Wall Street and with various firms, Marcus made the decision to start his own financial services company, Johnson Capital, LLC. Over the past several years, he has worked with more than 500 clients to help them choose, invest, and manage plans that will offer them the ability to truly prepare for their future.

As a financial planner, Marcus' main goal is to help his clients to make well-informed decisions on what types of investments are right for them. In his practice, he also emphasizes the need to adjust investment plans as your goals and needs change. Marcus will listen to your concerns and share information about potential investments including benefits, risks, and tax issues, and he will treat your financial goals with the same care and interest that he devotes to his own. Marcus looks forward to being your trusted advisor and expert resource as you build a secure portfolio of tailored solutions for your specific financial needs.

Marcus was awarded 40 under 40 by "Stay On The Go" magazine in Nashville, TN, and he is a member of the Chairman's Council. He was also the top life insurance producer in 2017. Marcus is also an accomplished jazz musician and has played in many places with a range of artists from Elle Varner to John Legend. He has an album on iTunes entitled "Passion Speaks Louder". Marcus and his wife Jamaria enjoy traveling, spending time with family, and also recording their Podcast entitled "Our House", which can also be found on iTunes.

JERRI EVANS

Independence Day
Jerri Evans

By my junior year of high school, I knew exactly what I wanted to be. I had my heart set on attending University of California Berkley. I was going to be an aeronautical engineer and become a "Cali girl." Many friends, family, teachers and even strangers asked me often,

"What college are you going to?" I hadn't even applied yet, let alone received an acceptance letter. But my response each time was consistent: "UC Berkley!" My guidance counselor suggested applying to multiple schools, so I did. I applied to Harvard, MIT, NYU, Florida Institute of Technology and University of Southern California.

Terri-Ann Jones, a TSU alum and my mother's co-worker at the time, asked,

"Jerri, did you apply to any HBCUs?"

"Nope, not interested."

She urged me to consider TSU. She even got me an invitation to Dr. Hefner's annual breakfast he hosted in Washington, D.C.

I remember to this day how excited the ambassadors were. They answered all the questions I had, even the unimportant ones like, "What are the boys like?" It was as if everyone was family, which, at the time, made me a bit apprehensive as a city kid. It was at that breakfast where I solidified a Presidential Scholarship to TSU. The rest has been history.

I entered TSU at the age of 17, and today, it's been 17 years since I set foot on TSU's campus. I've had the exact amount of time to apply everything I thought I knew back then. TSU is where I created lifelong relationships. Some of the best people I have ever met are from Memphis and Detroit. They taught me accountability, unconditional love, patience and relentlessness. They were my family away from family. They also helped me believe I was the greatest before I knew I was.

These same relationships show up for me in ways that I could never repay. We've been through marriages, births, divorces, deaths, grand openings, promotions, dance recitals and holidays. I couldn't tell you if the relationships I formed here could've been formed at a predominantly white university. What I am most sure of is that it wouldn't have been as colorful. TSU provided me a safe space to mature, a time to prepare, and a community that I will forever identify as my family.

"Enter to learn. Go forth to serve," now means so much more. Going into my seventh year of business, service has been a main pillar. In 2001, my mother, Annette Turner, was diagnosed with stage II breast cancer. For nine and a half years, my mother was in remission. Through lifestyle change, she remained healthy and became an advocate for healthy eating amongst our community. Southeast Washington, D.C. is historically known to be an underserved community. Having access to healthy options and better choices became my mission after losing my mom in 2010. Adding healthy options in communities that would otherwise lack it reminds me constantly of what TSU did for me. It built a bridge of where I was to what I needed and ultimately deserved. Turning Natural Juice Bars has become that oasis throughout the Washington, D.C. Metropolitan area. Serving cold-pressed juices, smoothies and vegan/vegetarian options at price points that are favorable to the patrons we serve.

I learned to hustle and align at TSU. While I studied engineering, I was afforded many opportunities to practice occasionally with my business hat. Mr. Richie, a director in the Mass Communication Department gave me an opportunity to plan and execute a homecoming concert. One of my most memorable experiences. I had no idea what I was doing and that was the beauty of it. To date, and I could be biased, but that was the best homecoming concert *ever*!

In those moments, I learned to be assertive, to respect budgets, and that managing people is difficult. These three things are at the height of what I do on a regular basis.

One of my favorite books, *Parable of the Sower* by Octavia Butler, says, "All that you touch you change. All that you change, changes you." TSU changed *me*. Now it's my turn to touch a few things, too, and change it for the better. Thank you, TSU. May every student, faculty member and employee continue to be better because of you.

About Jerri Evans

As the Owner of Turning Natural Juice Bars, Jerri Evans has revolutionized juicing in the hood. By bringing better choices to communities that otherwise lack access to healthy options, Jerri dedicated her mission to serving the under-served. Jerri has worked in the health and wellness industry with experience in Nutrition Education, Holistic Alternative Health, and more.

It was Evans' late mother Annette Turner, who founded Turning Natural, after being diagnosed with Stage II Breast Cancer. Sadly, after almost 10yrs living in remission, the disease returned and Annette fought her final fight in 2010. Shortly after her mother's transition, Evans quit her then excelling career as an Aeronautical Engineer to pursue helping those who were looking to take care of themselves.

As a hip hop aficionado pairing juices with the likes of her favorites Green Latifah, Swizz Beets, Bob Marley, Mi'Kale Jackson, and Just Blaze can all be found on recycled skateboards that serves as menu boards in store. Evans' personality can be found all throughout the stores, from the playlist, to the bookshelf, to art. 7 years and five locations later, Jerri has committed to continuing her mom's legacy and trailblazing her own.

.

ASHLEE OLIVER

Mo' Money

Ashlee Oliver

Attending an HBCU was a good decision. But attending Tennessee State University (TSU) was one of *the best decisions* I've made in my life. TSU is legendary for its family legacies and I, too, chose to attend TSU to continue in those footsteps that were formed by my cousins and fellow alumni: Michelle Fifer, Tonya Fifer, Cynthia Borrum-Matthews and extended family member, Derrica Brown. In addition to the school's rich culture, history and friends that become family along the way, the lessons and values you learn at TSU are priceless.

When I arrived on campus, the tall buildings that towered over me as I walked to class served as a beacon for me to strive for higher heights. I knew I had to be a light for others who would soon come behind me. It was at that moment that I said to myself, "Wow! I really made it to college!" Being accepted and making it to the campus was one thing. But my main goal was to finish with my BA in Business Information Systems.

Simply being on campus, walking around and figuring things out on my own was amazing. Kamadi Camp, Corey Smith and Gerald Bonaparte took me and other students on a "real college tour" during orientation. They gave us the blueprint of campus life, including the "Dos and Don'ts" of how to maintain a good reputation. Like many other students, during my freshman year, I quickly learned the true definition of being "purged." My classes had been purged. I quickly went to the financial aid office, where I was greeted by a long, dreadful line.

I met with my counselor and, luckily, we were able to get my schedule back to its original status. After that bizarre, yet pleasant experience, I knew where I wanted to work for the work study program. I instantly felt like an adult. TSU would be my home for four years, and that's where I started on the road to academic achievement, adulthood and major life achievements.

Living on campus was no place like home. I lived in Eppse Hall. Many mornings, bright and early, Ms. Hampton, the dorm director, came across the intercom loudly, addressing the issues at the dormitory.

"Ladies of Eppse Hall!" she would yell.

I couldn't believe my ears. I became angry because I was sleeping, but I learned to sleep through it.

I attended almost every event on campus, including plays, recitals, games, pep rallies, appreciation parties and talent shows. I was a contestant in many of the talent shows, too, including "The Battle of the Dorms." I was so excited, but the ladies who were performing with me were nervous.

They asked me, "Why aren't you nervous?"

"I always view everyone in the crowd as my fans. They're here for me!"

And it worked! After I gained notoriety, new friends and family came to support me at every show.

Although I was having the time of my life during my freshman year, I experienced a major setback during the second semester. I was diagnosed with *petite mal seizures.*

I had the first one in my dorm room late one night. I was extremely scared, so I called home and my mom calmed me down. Eventually, I fell asleep. I went to work study the next day and had a seizure much worse than the one I'd had the night before. Some of the staff assisted me during my crisis, and a family friend took me to the emergency room.

My eyes had been rolling in the back of my head for an hour. I had a headache. I was tired, confused, scared and ready for this fiasco to be over. I wasn't aptly diagnosed, so my family drove from Memphis to take me to the doctor at home. Cedria Hawk sat with me until they arrived. This was the start of a lifelong sisterhood. After a few days in the hospital, the doctor said, "Ms. Oliver, you are having petit mal seizures. You will not be able to drive for six months to a year. You have to take this prescription twice a day, every day, until the seizures stop."

I was devastated.

My family was scared, and they did not want me to return to TSU.

We went back and forth for a week or so, until I convinced them to let me return to my classes. I was ready to return to my grand college life at TSU. When I returned, my friends were so excited to see me. We were hanging out in the dorm room when I had yet another seizure. They didn't panic. They sat me down and made sure that I took my meds until it subsided. While I hated having to deal with seizures, it was a blessing to have friends who looked after me like family.

The seizures stopped in the fall. I was free to speak and to live my college life to the fullest again. *And I did just that!*

I went back to performing in talent shows and cultivating my love for music. I took Music Appreciation from the late great Dr. J.B. Howard. Unbeknownst to me, this groomed me for my future career as a DJ. Nearing graduation, I realized my legacy was already being written. I was one of the first grandchildren on my maternal side of the family to graduate from college. I was a graduate of The Tennessee State University Class of 2006! My grandmother, Ethel Mae Browning, was especially proud because she knew that no matter what I faced, I never gave up. Perseverance at its finest. I was blessed to turn my tassels to the right on my mother's birthday, December 16, 2006! It was an epic feeling.

But soon, reality set in. The fun and games were over, so to speak.

I was fortunate to land an internship the summer before graduation in my field. I was even able to return to the company as a contractor in March of 2007, which led to my full-time employment on December 16, 2008. I was so ecstatic that I cried a few tears of joy!

I worked diligently the next year and decided to deejay after purchasing a speaker for my family reunion. I bought more equipment as I landed more gigs. My business grew via word of mouth and social media, not to mention through family and friends who hired me. In 2014, I received a call to deejay for a group of alumni, "Da Crew TSU," for the homecoming tailgate. It is now one of my greatest joys to deejay at my HBCU! It gets better every year and my brand has truly blossomed.

My undergrad experience at TSU is the reason I come back every year. The people I met in undergrad are now part of my family. They greet me with love any time they see me. To be amongst some of the most influential, prestigious, successful, black college graduates is stupendous. TSU helped mold me into a productive, strategic, creative and successful computer software specialist and DJ! I appreciate everything this university has taught me.

Success is not given; it's earned!

I live by TSU's motto: Think. Work. Serve.

Think: Always use your mind, be strategic, plan and execute.

Work: Always out work the next person and work smarter.

Serve: Share your knowledge with those coming behind you. Be a blessing to others. Reach back and help them on your way up.

Overall, "The Land of Golden Sunshine" has made me humble, proud and appreciative of friends and family. It made me step outside my comfort zone. Working in the financial aid office made me patient. It made me want to help others and give them the tools to great success. Performing in the talent shows boosted my confidence as a DJ and entertainer. Our homecoming is not just a game; it's a family reunion. Singing the homecoming anthem, "Get geeked! Get geeked! It's homecoming week!" makes me even prouder. It's a language only my fellow alumni know and appreciate.

My cousin and fellow alumnus, Michelle Fifer, told me, "If you want to be remembered, set it in stone. Your mark will live forever!" Therefore,

I purchased a brick as a donation to the school, which reads: *Ashlee Oliver, A.O. The Great!* I left my legacy and my cousin Chardéa Harrison graduated from TSU in 2015. I hope, in the future, my nephew and other family members will carry the torch that I once held and keep it aflame!

Whether you attended Tennessee State University in the 1970s, or in 2020, the bond remains the same. Home is where the heart is, and my heart will forever bleed blue for my alma mater. History always speaks for itself. Let it speak for you as you, "Bring that college home." (Unknown)

About Ashlee Oliver

Ashlee Oliver (DJ A.O.) is a native Memphian, Tennessee State University (TSU) alumnus, and former member of The Association of Information Technology Professionals, AITT. After graduating Fall 2006 from the College of Business with a BA in Business Information Systems, Ashlee returned to Memphis and began her career as a Computer Software Specialist. Although her professional acumen has garnered her much respect in her field, it is her DJ for hire status that has gained her notoriety as a regional entertainer.

Meanwhile, TSU is credited for being the main stage that catapulted Ashlee's entertainment career when she entered as a freshman in July 2002. During the student orientation, the dorm director Ms. Hampton (Eppse Hall) and the students were moved by Ashlee's Freestyle Rapping, outgoing and witty personality. She performed in the battle of the dorms her freshman and sophomore year, in almost every talent show, and was featured on BET's Black College Tour. Ashlee began her DJ career in 2009 and it is growing immensely.

As a staunch supporter of her Alma Mater, in 2014 Ashlee began and continues to DJ the most Epic Tailgating Experience; hosted by a TSU Alum group known as 'Da Crew TSU', which is filmed by Loyalty Films(Johnathan Meadows). Ashlee Oliver, aka DJ A.O. has not only tailored her brand, but has also attended every TSU homecoming for the past 14 years! As a highly sought after, passionate professional, Ashlee brings the heat, an energetic musicality and her own style of diversity to the stage; while masterfully weaving hits, making lasting memories and spreading positive vibes and influence that will last a lifetime.

.

SHEMIKA DENISE BLOCKER

Life

Shemika Denise Blocker

The chorus to *All Roads Lead Home* by Ohana Bam immediately comes to mind when I think about my HBCU experience. It all began with my dream of attending Tennessee State University to become a part of the pre-med program. My single, hard-working mom could not understand why her child, who had full scholarships to multiple schools in Alabama, just *had to* attend Tennessee State University. But regardless of her lack of understanding, she still drove me up Highway 65 North, in what we considered to be a snowstorm, to Tennessee State University.

We had to wait to speak with the president of the university, whom we did not have a scheduled appointment with. Talk about courage. We waited around until President Hefner was available. When he was, I presented him with my academic and extracurricular resume from high school, highlighting the fact that I graduated number two in my class. After a lengthy conversation turned interview, I was awarded an out-of-state tuition waiver. Boy, how I wish I had appreciated that waiver a little more down the road.

Freshman year, I was finally on the campus of Tennessee State University. There were so many nice people from various organizations outside of Wilson Hall (one of the female freshman residence halls) to help us move in. Some even offered me a ride to Walmart to stock my room with anything that would aid in the gain of the Freshman 15! Once I was all moved in, and mom had gone back to Alabama, it really hit me that I was alone. For the first time in eighteen years, this only child was finally alone and away from home.

Classes were in session. I attended them, except for the ones that fell on "Wonderful Wednesday." For some odd reason, I did not do homework. So much so that I didn't pass all my classes, which I thought would be okay—until I went to register for my spring semester classes.

I registered, but no sooner than I registered was I purged out of them. I lost my out-of-state tuition waiver, which made paying for school a reality that I was not prepared to face. Having to tell my mom that her once studious daughter had played around her first semester of school surely would point to all roads leading home, straight down 65 South. So, I couldn't let her know. I went from the financial aid line to the bursar's office, back to financial aid. I went back and forth until we figured out how to keep me in school, without my mom knowing anything.

Going into spring semester, I quickly learned that college was truly preparation for life. The same rules applied. The statement, "It's all in who you know," held just as much weight then as it does now in the professional world. Once I learned that, my spring semester motivation still was not academics. I learned how to get involved in organizations that served a purpose, while also connecting with the right people. One would think that I pulled it together after that first semester scare, right? Nope! This time I actually went to class and did the homework while trying to balance being involved in other organizations and networking. However, that landed me back in the same position at the end of the semester—struggling academically, which was a lane I was *not* accustomed to being in.

I went home that summer and pretended that all was well. I knew I had to figure something out quickly because, at this point, all roads didn't have to lead home. I was already there for the summer and could have simply stayed. A lot of silent prayers went out that summer because I couldn't tell my mom. I couldn't come home for good. I had a couple of family members who didn't want me to succeed and I had to prove them wrong. Lo and behold, some of those connections I spent time making in the spring paid off. I landed an interview to become a resident assistant in the honors co-ed residence hall on campus my sophomore year. This meant that room and board were covered for that entire school year. Now, I had to do my part and hold down my grades. I also had to maintain my new position, which I took very seriously.

Sophomore year was, by far, my favorite year of my undergraduate experience. I was more involved, more focused, more vocal and more courageous that year. Yet, that was the year that caused me the most heartache. I was so busy trying to be involved that I was not busy enough maintaining the main qualification it took to become a member of the first and finest African-American Greek sorority: *my grade point average.* I learned that it does not matter how many people you know or how cool you are. If your grades are crap, people cannot vouch for you. I experienced that firsthand. I understood it; yet it still didn't change the level of devastation and embarrassment. It was so much that I wanted to go home, but I stuck it out. I pulled myself together. Everyone who was rooting for me were still rooting for me. Yet, they were more on my ass about getting it together, full circle.

Junior and senior year, I finally got my stride. I, unfortunately, had that whole student loan thing figured out, as well as my connections in high places. So, if the aroma of purging was in the atmosphere, I was ready. At this point, I had experienced working and living off campus, as well as working a work study job and living in on-campus apartments.

I had four years of different living experiences. I had experienced seasons of thinking that certain semesters would be my last semester. I experienced rejection and acceptance. I experienced coming into college with one set of buddies and leaving out with new ones. I had experienced the passing of loved ones and having to support friends enduring the same. I had experienced life, love and lessons that I would have never experienced had I allowed those challenges to create roads to lead me home.

I will forever be willing to share with the incoming freshman who have no clue about all the things college has to offer. I also had this pretty dope female sister/friend in my life during those years who saw things in me that others did not see. She saw that I was making strides in the right direction, but she knew no graduate program would take me seriously leaving undergraduate with less than a 3.0 GPA. So, I stayed an additional year to pull it all the way together and I graduated with a 3.2 GPA. I decided to take a year off, but I went back and obtained a master's degree, graduating with a 3.75 GPA with that same sister/friend's voice in my ear rooting for me!

So initially, "All roads lead home" meant this Bama girl taking a hike back down 65 South. She couldn't get her stuff together. But, in hindsight, the experiences, the fears, the tears were all a part of her journey to truly plant her feet in the Land of Golden Sunshine by the Cumberland's fertile shore because *this is home.*

All roads led to Tennessee State University. TSU. I am she. She is me. I am who I am because she challenged me to be! I would not change any part of my journey. Go, Big Blue!

About Shemika Denise Blocker

Shemika Denise is a from Birmingham, AL. In 2003, she moved to Nashville, TN to attend THE Tennessee State University where she majored in Biology with a minor in Chemistry. After being a part of various service organizations and volunteering at places like Martha O' Bryan and the Boys and Girls Club, Shemika began questioning her path. She was on a path to pediatric medicine but saw the need to serve and aid in the low-income communities in the form of education for children who were not on grade level, lacked support, sometimes food and access to high quality education. At the time of her great epiphany, it was far too late to change her major so she decided to get a Masters in Social Work from The University of Tennessee focusing on Management, Leadership, and Community Practice. Subsequently, she began working with nonprofits and the charter school sector.

Shemika currently serves staff, students, and families as a School Operations Manager for the largest charter school network in Nashville, TN. She is responsible for the day to day operations of the school excluding instruction and culture. In addition to her love for her career, Shemika's first love is her incredible nine-year-old daughter, Skye Daleigha. Skye keeps her busy with their mother daughter activities, in addition to her extracurricular schedule with basketball, volleyball, and dance. Skye is the reason Shemika continues to strive for greatness.

AIRIELLE VINCENT

Crooklyn

Airielle Vincent

Your family teaches you a lot about yourself.

Even when their embarrassing stories and drama make me want to run away, I am still grateful for them. I'm grateful for the person they helped mold me into today. I have learned several lessons from my family. The top three that relate to my passion for teaching at an HBCU include:

First, education is imperative.

Second, you will always be confronted with challenges; but you must overcome each obstacle that could potentially stop your progress.

Third, if you want to see change, be the change maker, not the one who sits back and complains.

Let's begin with education. From preschool to my doctoral program, I have attended predominantly white schools. I am accustomed to carving out black space in a white world. I remember being in rooms, worrying if other students assumed that I was a "token minority" or if I only made it because of affirmative action. My family constantly reminded me that I was in school to learn, not to worry about what others thought.

My grandmother was born in Mississippi in 1929, during a time when black farms were stolen by whites who threatened to lynch any black who questioned them. Many families, including my own, had to escape to the north for safety and for jobs. My grandmother was one of ten children. Even though she gained acceptance to Spelman College, her family told her that they didn't have enough money for her to attend. Only one out of the ten siblings could attend college. My great aunt attended a Historically Black College and University (HBCU) to obtain her nursing degree. She became the first African American nurse anesthetist in the city of Detroit. Her husband went to Meharry Medical School, which was the only school for black doctors.

Even without a college education, my grandmother started her own extermination company in the city of Detroit out of the trunk of her car. She became one of very few African American women in the city of Detroit to own and operate a business. She also was the first female president of The Pest Control Association. My mother, Carolyn Clifford, is a 17-time Emmy Award-winning journalist who is a news anchor in Detroit. She attended Michigan State University. While in school, she was one of a handful of blacks in the dance company, ROTC and the Pom-Pom team. She was also one of few blacks in many classrooms, including her journalism courses. Those experiences taught her how to succeed in the news industry. Throughout her career, she has always been one of a handful of African Americans in the newsrooms. Being called "the N word" taught her that although racism exists, you must rise above it. You must succeed, despite those around you who would prefer you fail. It's been her mission, and she's taught me that if you succeed, reach back and pull an African American forward with you. That is what I'm doing as a professor at an HBCU that produced the most successful African American woman in the world: Oprah Winfrey. I am giving back and pulling students forward who need a hand up, not a handout!

Next, we move to confronting challenges.

My first challenge after gaining an education was forging my path. I used to wonder why anyone would choose a career that requires long, difficult work hours, quick deadlines and working on holidays or through snowstorms. But that's the life of a journalist. Whether you are in front of the camera, behind the scenes, or at a newspaper or magazine, when you've been bitten by the news bug, you're hooked. If it's your true passion, your dedication never waivers.

For me, it started when I was young. I grew up in a newsroom, watching my mother work every shift in the business. On weekends, my brother and I would pack up our sleeping bags and games and we hung out at the television station where my mom worked tirelessly. She tackled every job

174

imaginable—from writing and editing, to producing. Back then, I thought this couldn't possibly be the road I would follow. But I soon realized that the bug that strikes every journalist was lingering throughout my life. Telling stories and communicating with others run through my veins, giving me the necessary juice to tackle the ever-changing world of the news industry.

I have worked in many different newsrooms. I've celebrated winning Emmy Awards, AP Awards and a regional Edward R. Murrow Award with my family. However, I knew something was missing. I didn't recognize it at first. But, through every job and career change, communication skills, writing and, most importantly, inspiring others has been at the forefront. Working in the news business prepared me to teach future journalists to excel in the business. Teaching is my passion. I truly believe God put me on this path to *make change*.

Finally, I'm committed to be a change agent.

Teaching at an HBCU gives my life purpose and meaning. I love teaching younger generations that they, too, can succeed, despite life's challenges. I love seeing a student's eyes light up when given an opportunity to learn during an internship, or when we bring in company representatives who give them potential job leads. I love to hear firsthand, "Thank you for making me believe and for showing me that I have a clear path forward in the job market."

My purpose and mission at Tennessee State University is clear. Teaching at Tennessee State University has connected me to my lineage as a black academic advisor, and it's helped me further understand what students of color are struggling with in higher learning institutions and in corporate America. This experience allows me to be a change maker in and around our community. It's a privilege to be a part of an institution that is dedicated to empowering people who look like me.

About Airielle Vincent

Airielle Vincent is an award-winning news producer turned educator, backed by a combined 10+ years of academic and practical experience in media and marketing. She's won an AP award for Best TV Evening Newscast, an Emmy award for Best Newscast, and a Regional Edward R. Murrow Award.

Airielle is currently an Assistant Professor facilitating courses in Integrated Marketing Communications at Tennessee State University. She brings expertise in management and marketing. Vincent takes pride in identifying teaching needs and measuring training effectiveness in the classroom. Her research expertise centers around social media policies and strategies and how to reduce negative attention and enhance organizational reputations.

In her spare time, Airielle runs a small social media management business. She works with brand influencers like HBCU Go and sports organizations like Global Coach. Airielle produces and co-hosts two shows on Sirius XM. She recently published her first novella, *I Used To Know Him*.

JOSCELYNE BRAZILE

Strictly Business
Joscelyne Brazile

"The world is not all black, why should my college be?" I found myself choking on those words during a lunchtime debate that no one had challenged me to. It was just a month before high school graduation, and I was committed to joining most of my friends in a college town on a full scholarship to a predominantly white institution (PWI). I knew intimately the value of an education at a Historically Black College or University (HBCU); my entire family was educated through an HBCU. Why, then, had I decided to attack their college experiences to validate my own decisions?

As an adult, I can affirm that it is because insecurities are loud. I still can't, however, articulate exactly why I had chosen that institution. However, on April 16, 1998, Tennessee State University *chose me*. That's the day a tornado touched down in the middle of my campus tour. It's also the day that a chance encounter with Dr. James A. Hefner, president of Tennessee State University—and a sticky note—changed the course of my life. Someone asked me to give the sticky note to the TSU Foundation Office, which simply read: "Gibson. President Full." Just two weeks after that chance meeting, the illegible message I'd carried to the TSU Foundation Office materialized into a package outlining a full-scholarship opportunity to attend TSU.

I had no idea how life was about to open for me. Prior to landing in Nashville, I lived in the same home in my hometown my entire life. Nashville, was, indeed, a *different world*. I was enthralled by all of it, from the live music and bright lights of scenic downtown that danced across the Cumberland River, to the curated confidence of the women who graced the campus. This place had so much knowledge to lend to a bright-eyed, optimistic girl from Jacksonville, Florida. I was ready to absorb as much of it as my heart could hold. I was in love.

I arrived at Tennessee State University, knowing no one. I didn't know much about the campus culture. I'd met one fellow freshman while cheering at a National Bowl Game in Hawaii. By the time my family trekked from Florida to Wilson Hall, it was late. I had no interest in meeting anyone or spending my first night in "The Zoo." When I arrived, that cheerleader, and three of her friends from Benton Harbor, Michigan, were waiting at my dorm room to help me unpack. Those same friends, upon learning that I didn't own a winter coat, took me shopping to make sure I was prepared for the coming fall months and winter. Those women taught me to trust women.

At orientation, I was prepared to engage in the cliché of looking to my left and my right in anticipation of being told that one of the men or women next to me would not return the following semester. Instead, students who filled the seats in the auditorium were powerfully charged with the challenge to wake up running. The message that was repeated so many times during our matriculation inspired strangers to become friends, and friends to become family. We were a collective of students from diverse backgrounds who found themselves charting the same path together. We learned how to win together.

In addition to learning how to win together, professors in and out of the classroom challenged us to challenge ourselves in thought, word and deed. As we pursued our individual courses of study from economics to engineering, we were engaged in a parallel journey of tearing down the mental constructs and assumptions that our respective decades of pre-college education once built. We were re-learning who we were and what we were capable of.

We were also learning to use our gifts to help one another win. During a particularly rigorous math course, I recall surveying the room to gauge understanding. With the exception of one other student, a football player, understanding was lost in the thick Russian accent of our very enthusiastic professor. Without discussion, two students got up and headed to the front of the class to help our classmates. Twenty years later, I still count that football player as my best friend and the father of my goddaughter.

In addition to learning the power of collective wins, we learned the collective power of loss. The college president who changed my life with a sticky note has made his transition to heaven, as have classmates that left

180

their Tiger prints on the hearts of many. The gift of Dr. Hefner's legacy is that, in loss, we look to our left and to our right, and we challenge one another to continue to *wake up running* when one of us doesn't return. What we now know, twenty years later, is that perseverance through loss is how we get to the wins. Those wins, though bittersweet, are wrapped in the love and legacies of those who fell so that we can keep running.

Every day that I wake up running, I honor the college experiences of those who surrendered their own college experiences to activism so that I could safely and freely enjoy the best academic experience of my life. My parents attended HBCUs during The Civil Rights Movement. My father was in Montgomery, Alabama when Dr. Martin Luther King, Jr. was assassinated. The privilege to attend Tennessee State University on the shoulders of Freedom Riders and the luminaries of the 1990 Student Government Association endowed me with a charge to lead. Student government activists, just eight years prior to my arrival on campus, fought for the campus I enjoyed and still call my second home. Thus, I treated my HBCU experience as a love letter in response to a sticky note signed in 1998 by the legends who came before me.

I understood the neutrality of time when I arrived at TSU. I had four years to fit my entire college experience into that timeframe. I chose to study economics. I became a member of the Alpha Psi Chapter of Alpha Kappa Alpha. I worked on campaigns for people who I believed in. I engaged in political processes. I explored pathways to find and use my voice.

In retrospect, every day that I spent on that campus, exploring, observing, asking questions, accepting challenges and engaging in conversations, meant more than choosing a career path or a college major. My HBCU experience taught me that time is a gift. My HBCU experience was a gift.

Over twenty-two years after accepting the gift of my HBCU experience on a sticky note from the president of TSU, I count myself lucky to create these same opportunities for so many deserving students who aspire to attend HBCUs. My life's work builds on a legacy of passionate educators who aspire to change lives, just as my life was changed. As a scholar and top performer, TSU ignited in me a passion for scholarship and making collegiate experiences a gift to others.

I didn't choose my HBCU; TSU chose me. For that, I am forever grateful. Since receiving a scholarship to TSU, I have taken pride in choosing my alma mater with every gift, every mentoring opportunity, every answered phone call, every chance airport encounter with alumni and students, and every visit back to campus. I chose the path my parents laid through their sacrifices. I chose the friendships that became family. I choose to leave my legacy in scholarship support for future Tigers. I choose to love and support TSU in grateful appreciation for choosing me.

About Joscelyne Brazile

Joscelyne M. Brazile is a researcher, fundraiser, and a scholar in the areas of burnout, activism, philanthropy and leadership. She has been a professional fundraiser for over twelve years and is passionate about the HBCU collegiate experience. She also serves as a Board Member and Advisor for a number of causes devoted to the advancement of African and African-American culture.

Previously, Joscelyne worked for UNC-Chapel Hill in the areas of Centers & Institutes, Medicine and Merit-Based scholarship programs. Her career launched in the political arena and shifted to higher education after completing a Master of Science from DePaul University. She is also a proud graduate of Tennessee State University.

Born and raised in Jacksonville, FL, Joscelyne now enjoys calling Durham, NC home. She loves spending time with family and friends exploring the many sights and sounds Bull City has to offer. A new adventure is never far away – Joscelyne is more than halfway to her goal of visiting all 50 U.S. States. Her career in advancement is inspired by her own college experience, which she hopes to pay forward a million times over.

BROOKE KIMBRO-SCOTT

Training Day

Brooke Kimbro-Scott

"Are you serious? Why did you do that?"

I came from an academic magnet school. I could not believe this was happening to me.

It was the very first assignment in my Business Orientation class, not to mention my first semester of my freshman year at Tennessee State University (TSU). I'd just graduated from Martin Luther King, Jr. Magnet High School in Nashville with a 3.9 GPA. I was studious, focused, diligent and determined to start college off right.

But this was not what I had envisioned.

The margin was properly aligned. There was precise spacing between lines and the paragraphs were perfect. I followed all the instructions. I checked and doubled checked the spelling. I ensured that the staple was in the proper place.

I used the essay formula that I'd learned in high school. And I poured my heart and soul out on the topic. I knew this would guarantee me an A+.

Dr. James Ellzy was a tall, slender man who always dressed in a suit and wore glasses. He had the demeanor and mannerisms of President Barack Obama. He was the chair of the Department of Business Information Systems (BIS) and professor of BIS. At the time, my major was finance. But, little did I know, I would change my major to BIS after my freshman year due to an enlightened experience I had at an internship that summer.

Dr. Ellzy spoke with distinction. He clearly articulated his thoughts and points. This was one professor I immediately admired. I knew I would learn a lot from him. It was Dr. Ellzy who initially exposed me to the concept of what it meant to produce excellence at TSU.

He called for everyone to walk to the front of the class and turn in their papers on the desk. I waited a while to stand, but then happily proceeded to the front. I was the last student to place my assignment on the stack. After everyone sat at their desks, Dr. Ellzy looked at the stack in silence. He picked up my paper and flipped through the pages. He looked up at the class with a stern stare, then proceeded to rip up my assignment in two. He tossed it in the trash next to the desk. He took the next two papers and did the same thing.

I thought to myself, *Surely, this man is crazy! He doesn't know who I am!* Before I could get a word out, he explained.

"While I am sure some of you did a great job on content and followed the instructions, that's still not good enough. As college students, you're embarking on a high level of education and should think differently. Think twice about the next assignment to determine if it will be at this level of excellence."

This experience was just the first of many times that TSU stretched me to reevaluate what excellence really meant. TSU put everyone on the same starting line. It didn't matter whether your paper was A+ or F material. It was a new day to give even more than we'd ever given before. This race would be different than any other race we'd run before. Dr. James A. Hefner also had a similar message for students.

Throughout my tenure at TSU, he reminded us, "Every morning in Africa, a gazelle wakes up. It knows it must outrun the fastest lion or it will be killed. Every morning in Africa, a lion wakes up. It knows it must run faster than the slowest gazelle or it will starve. It doesn't matter whether you're the lion or the gazelle. When the sun comes up, you'd better be running." Excellence was the new normal. Little did I know, this would shape and develop me academically throughout my college career at TSU— and the rest of my life.

TSU pushed me in many other ways, as well. Henry Kimbro was one of the great Negro league baseball players from 1937 to 1953. In 1946, Kimbro hit for a .376 average against the competition. The next season was

.363. Henry Kimbro was my grandfather. He was one of the people, along with my father, Phillip Kimbro, who inspired me to play softball. I was never as good as my grandfather. But with coaching from my father and others, I managed to make all-star teams in the competitive leagues around Nashville and played for my high school. I love this sport!

When I decided to try out for the Tennessee State University Women's Softball Team my freshman year, I was the only walk-on to make the team. I received the #29 jersey. This was an accomplishment within itself, as all the rest of my teammates were there on scholarships. The team was aiming for the championships. As a magnet high school, our softball program was not one of the highest ranked in Nashville. While we played well as a team, and we ranked competitively in our division, we never experienced the rigor and conditioning practices of a highly ranked program. I was in for a rude awakening of what it would take to be a part—and stay a part—of this team.

When approaching the TSU Gentry Center Complex from the back road, I couldn't help but notice that the center sits on a large hill. On a clear day, I could see the rolling hills of Tennessee in the far distance. I could also see the TSU Tigers softball and track fields. Since the hill was very steep, there are 80 to 100 steps to get down to the fields and back up to the center.

It was early August when we started to practice. The track team next door had been practicing since the summer. Before we started practice in the afternoons, I used to watch them condition. I used to run hurdles in middle school, so I was amazed at the skills the Tigerbelles displayed and the type of conditioning they had to go through. For a walk-on, I was doing good. I proved that I had valuable batting skills and descent outfield techniques. Later that August,

I experienced another game-changing moment that caused me to, again, rethink the meaning of excellence.

We started weight training in early mornings and late evenings before practice. This took some getting used to, but I did a good job waking up at 5 a.m. for weights. I was taking 18 hours of classes, and then I'd head to practice and more weights three out of five days a week. The challenge came when our coach asked us to start a new conditioning program: the hill. This was the same hill outside the Gentry Center. I watched the track team run up and down this hill before and after their practices. For us, if a team member stopped running the hill, the entire team would have to run several laps around the perimeter of the softball field.

My first run, post-practice, didn't go as planned. On the way down the hill, after four cycles, my legs started to go numb. Eventually, they gave out. I quickly got back up, but I could not move. Crying, yet still determined to finish, I even tried to crawl to no avail. Our coach had to carry me down the hill. The embarrassment, disappointment and physical pain I felt was unreal. I couldn't believe I'd failed and let my team down. I was devastated.

After the team ran several laps around the field, something happened that I didn't expect. Instead of crazy looks and curses, everyone said, "It will be okay. You'll make it next time."

At that moment, I knew I was a part of something great. That year, we won the most games ever in our conference since 1994, but we lost at the OVC championships. We had achieved a new level of excellence, though.

I had many more experiences and opportunities for growth and perseverance throughout my matriculation at TSU. I joined one of the greatest sororities in The Divine Nine, Zeta Phi Beta Sorority, Inc. I received the USAA All-American Scholar, joined the Golden Key National Honor Society and Beta Gamma Sigma Business Honor Society. I studied abroad and graduated magna cum laude with a BBA in Business Information Systems, all while working and holding several internships all four years. I learned to push through and give all I had to give and more. TSU created a strong foundation of excellence that I continue to expand today. I'm so glad I went to TSU!

About Brooke Kimbro-Scott

Brooke Kimbro-Scott is a solutions-oriented and versatile IT professional possessing over 15 years of experience that includes program/project management, digital transformation, and cross-functional team leadership. As a Digital Technology Manager, Brooke is responsible for leading the global implementation of Caterpillar Financial's digital transformation vision and strategy through identified projects and agile initiatives.

Brooke is a native of Nashville and holds an MBA in Leadership from Lipscomb University and bachelor's degree in Business Information Systems from Tennessee State University. She is an active participant on the Advisory Board of Tennessee State University College of Business, Tennessee State University National Alumni Association, and a member of Zeta Phi Beta Sorority Incorporated. She is also a recipient of the 2019 Nashville Emerging Leader Award for Technology. Her 11-year-old daughter is a published author of a children's book called Talking Planets. Brooke enjoys international travel, cycling, games, and activities with her daughter.

KYNDALL LEWIS

Down in the Delta

Kyndall Lewis

As I woke up, the sunlight beamed through the gaps of the curtains. Bacon, pancakes and eggs filled the house with the most comforting southern aroma.

"Kyndall Pooh! Lori Lu! Time to get up." My cousin Lori and I ran into the kitchen where my mom was cooking breakfast.

"Look at my sugar lumps!" Paw Paw shouted as he helped us to our seats at the table.

We could do no wrong in our grandfather's eyes. I was so excited. It was parade and game day! Most of my mom's family graduated from Mississippi Valley State University in Itta Bena, Mississippi. Every year, my family got together to go to homecoming. Little did I know at seven years old that homecoming was just getting started for me. As we pulled up in downtown Greenwood, Mississippi, we secured our spot on the street to see all the bands, to wave at the queen and catch candy! It was like Christmas in October. I knew then that an HBCU was in my future. Fast forward to eleven years later. I started my freshman year at Tennessee State University!

Never in a million years did I think I'd attend Tennessee State University. Yes, I was going to college. Yes, I was going to an HBCU. But TSU? No. Being from Memphis, Tennessee, I attended the Southern Heritage Classic annually. The Southern Heritage Classic is a Memphis holiday. All the black people get together to tailgate and watch Tennessee State University take on Jackson State University. I felt like I saw TSU every year, so I didn't want to enroll there. I also graduated from Whitehaven High School, where it seemed like *everyone* went to TSU. I even called TSU "Whitehaven University" at one point.

When I started my senior year of high school, I had a long conversation with one of my favorite teachers, Ms. Tangela Taylor, affectionately known

191

as "TT." Oddly enough, she did not actually teach me. But I worked on her prom committee for two years and she couldn't get rid of me! I sat in her classroom and explained how I could not narrow my decision down. TSU wasn't even on my list! I applied just so I could add it to my acceptance letter list. I didn't think I'd actually attend. Well, TT talked about her experience. As she talked, it became nostalgic for me. Her stories made me think of the homecomings at MVSU. She even promised to provide me with a list of people working at TSU to contact if I decided to attend. I thought long and hard, and I decided that I would go visit. I told myself if I liked what I saw, I would go. Well, anybody who has been to TSU can tell you that the campus is absolutely beautiful. Everyone was so welcoming, and it seemed as if they were thriving. It did something to my soul to see young, black people handling business and bettering themselves. Everyone was full of life! After TT's talk and that campus visit, I, too, fell in the "Big Blue" trap. Thank God I did!

The beauty of being from Memphis and going to TSU was that there was always somebody you knew from home in the mix. After the first few weeks, I was in love with TSU!

I couldn't see myself going anywhere else! I thoroughly enjoyed being around like-minded individuals from all over the world. Freshman year was all about getting my feet wet and living the authentic college life with my friends from home, while connecting with new friends. It was crazy how easy it was to form relationships in college. It was nothing like high school. Everyone was into networking and hanging out. By the time I completed one full day on campus, I had at least three new friends. After connecting with so many people my freshman year, I set my sights on being more involved on campus. As a sophomore, I became a TSU Tiger Gem and a member of the National Association of Colored Women's Clubs Incorporated-Women of Empowerment, The Frankie J. Pierce Federated Chapter, under the direction of Ms. Eleanor Bass. As a member of the 26 Keys in NACWC, I formed many relationships that continue to thrive today.

In the fall of my junior year, I became a member of Alpha Kappa Alpha Sorority, Incorporated, the Awesomely Sophisticated Alpha Psi Chapter.

Being in Alpha Psi helped me create a bond with so many dynamic women. I always knew I would be a member of Alpha Kappa Alpha; it is part of my family's legacy. What I did not realize was that, through Alpha Psi alone, I would gain a new family. As far as siblings go, I have one brother and no sisters. By the time I left TSU, I had over 100 sisters, all from Alpha Psi. The bond is undeniably amazing and unmatched. Meeting so many members of Alpha Psi and staying connected to them throughout the years has been nothing short of a pleasure. I have a set of sisters who will forever be my family.

My most unforgettable experience at Tennessee State University was the presidential election of 2008. For me, it was a double luxury. I was 18 and it was the first time I exercised my right to vote. On top of that, I was part of history—electing the first black president of the United States of America. It was Tuesday, November 4, 2008. TSU planned an election watch party in Kean Hall. Of course, this was a huge deal. For the first time in American history, there was a strong possibility that the president of the United States would be a black man, Barack Obama. As the votes came in, it hurt to see that Tennessee was a Republican state. However, we were all hopeful and anxious at the same time. You could hear people talk about how they thought America would change for the better with a black president. It was so exciting. Just to be around and in a collegiate setting at that time was an amazing feeling. As we sat on the edge of our seats and bit our fingernails, the votes were in! CNN announced that Barack Obama was the 44th President of the United States of America and America's first black president.

I can still hear the screams of excitement and see the hype that filled Kean Hall that night. Our SGA president at the time made a speech like he had just been elected. He told us we were walking to Fisk to celebrate. We left Kean Hall and headed toward Fisk University. Seeing the crowd walk to Fisk was *unbelievable*. For a split second, I understood the sense of pride our ancestors had when they marched on Washington. We chanted all the way there, while cars on the street blasted Young Jeezy's new song, *My President*. It felt like I was in a scene out of *A Different World*!

TSU is only about a five-minute drive to Fisk University, so it didn't take long for us to get there on foot. We made it to Fisk and both SGA Presidents stood together. They spoke on how this was a win for *us*, for the *black community*. To see both HBCUs come together to celebrate the victory of putting Barack Obama in office was one of the most memorable moments—not only at Tennessee State University—but also in my life. I will never forget that experience.

Another reason that attending an HBCU, *my HBCU*, was the only option was because of the homecoming experience. TSU has one of the best homecoming experiences. Homecoming as a TSU student was fun. But as an alum, *it's incredible*. Coming back once a year to celebrate TSU is like a highly anticipated family reunion. There is an unexplainable gratification seeing people who once walked the campus with you mature and prosper. Homecoming is your platform to brag, while congratulating others. It's a time to be unapologetically fly and overdressed. It's the time to turn up, like you're still a college student and reconnect with old friends! I think that's what makes TSU so special to me: the family-oriented environment. I truly have gained a TSU family that is irreplaceable and constantly growing. Whenever I come across a TSU graduate, we scream with excitement and hug like we've known each other for years! Being a TSU alumnus means being part of an exclusive tribe. I hope and pray that when I start a family, at least one of my children will consider Tennessee State University. Being part of its legacy has been one of the best decisions I made in my life.

In the beginning, I didn't even want to go to TSU. I thank God I did.

About Kyndall Lewis

Kyndall's *"Grit & Grind"* comes naturally as she maneuvers through life. A native Memphian and graduate of Whitehaven High School, her passion for Memphis runs deep! Kyndall received her bachelor's degree in Fashion Merchandising from Tennessee State University, allowing her to gain styling and merchandising experience with Forever 21, Bebe Stores, and Lacoste. While building her fashion resume she decided to take her talents to the classroom. For three years, Kyndall taught Family and Consumer Science at Melrose High School in the historical Orange Mound neighborhood of Memphis, Tennessee. It was there that Kyndall quickly discovered her passion for children and working to make a positive impression on the community. Student and community advocate by day and entrepreneur by night, Kyndall currently serves as the Student & Community Resource Associate for a redevelopment project in Memphis, Tennessee; while fostering her creative empire, The Monreaux Method.

Tennessee State University
Fun Facts

In 1909, the Tennessee State General Assembly created three normal schools, including the Agricultural and Industrial Normal School, which would grow to become TSU.
(http://www.tnstate.edu/about_tsu/history.aspx)

The first 247 students began their academic careers on June 19, 1912. William Jasper Hale served as head of the school of The Tennessee Agricultural and Industrial State Normal School for Negroes.
(http://www.tnstate.edu/about_tsu/history.aspx)

The Agricultural and Industrial Normal School gained the capacity to grant bachelor's degrees in 1922.
(http://www.tnstate.edu/about_tsu/history.aspx)

By 1924, the college became known as The Tennessee Agricultural and Industrial State Normal College and the first degrees were awarded. In 1927, "Normal" was dropped from the name.
(http://www.tnstate.edu/about_tsu/history.aspx)

President William Jasper Hale retired in 1943, after 32 years of service.
(http://www.tnstate.edu/about_tsu/history.aspx)

Walter S. Davis, an alumnus of A&I School, was selected as the second president in 1943. He oversaw significant expansion of the college during his tenure until his retirement in 1968.
(http://www.tnstate.edu/about_tsu/history.aspx)

The first master's degrees were awarded in June of 1944.
(http://www.tnstate.edu/about_tsu/history.aspx)

Under the name Tennessee Agricultural & Industrial State University, the institution achieved full land-grant university status in August of 1958.
(http://www.tnstate.edu/about_tsu/history.aspx)

Another TSU alumnus, Andrew Torrence, was named the university's third president after Walter Davis retired as president in 1968. The state legislature dropped "Agricultural & Industrial" and officially changed the name to Tennessee State University.
(http://www.tnstate.edu/about_tsu/history.aspx)

James Hefner became TSU's sixth president in 1991 and fostered enrollment growth to an all-time high of 9,100 students.
(http://www.tnstate.edu/about_tsu/history.aspx)

In the university's 100-year history, Dr. Glenda Baskin Glover became president in January of 2013, as well as the International President of Alpha Kappa Alpha Sorority, Inc. in 2018. She's also one of two African-American women to hold the PhD-CPA-JD combination in the nation.
(http://www.tnstate.edu/about_tsu/history.aspx)

The College of Engineering has a corporate partnership with NASA, Raytheon and General Motors.
(https://en.wikipedia.org/wiki/Tennessee_State_University)

Former TSU Track & Field Coach, Ed Temple, who was the head coach of two Olympic teams, was selected as a member of the 2012 class of the U.S. Olympic Hall of Fame.
(http://www.tnstate.edu/about_tsu/history.aspx)

John A. Merritt Blvd (1982) and the John Merritt Classic (1999) are named after one of TSU's most well-known head football coaches during his 20-year tenure – "Big John" Merritt.
(http://www.tsutigers.com/athletics/history/)

TSU Tiger Spotlight

Thelma Harper – Member of Tennessee Senate (1989-2019)
Brenda Gilmore – Member of Tennessee Senate (2019-Present)
Harvey Johnson, Jr. – Mayor of Jackson, MS (1997-2005; 2009-2013)
A. C. Wharton – Mayor of Memphis, TN (2009-2015)
Bobby Jones – Gospel Music Singer and Television Host

Anthony Levine – Baltimore Ravens
Robert Covington – Houston Rockets
Dominique Rodgers-Cromartie – Washington Redskins
Clint Gray, EJ Reed and Derrick Moore – Owners of Slim & Husky's and The Roll Out
Robert Higgins – Owner of Minerva Ave. and Partner of WKND Hang Suite

Hall of Famers

The National Black College Alumni Hall of Fame Foundation, Inc.

Arts & Entertainment

1996 - Oprah Winfrey, Tennessee State University

2003 - Dr. Bobby Jones, Tennessee State University

Athletics

1995 - Ralph Boston, Tennessee State University

2005 - Wyomia Tyus, Tennessee State University

2009 - Edith McGuire-Duvall, Tennessee State University

Business and Industry

2009 - Dr. Theophilus Boyd, III, Tennessee State University

(Business)

Civil Rights Award

2011 - Freedom Riders, Tennessee State University

Community Service

1992 - Xernona Clayton, Tennessee State University

Faith and Theology

2007 - Rev. Dr. Gerald Durley, Tennessee State University

Government and Law

2008 - General Lloyd "Fig" Newton, Ret., Tennessee State University (Government)

2010 - Honorable Curtis L. Collier, Tennessee State University (Law)

Medicine

2004 - Dr. Levi Watkins, Tennessee State University

2007 - Dr. Alvin H. Crawford, Tennessee State University

Lifetime Achievement

1996 - Edward Stanley Temple, Tennessee State University

Official Partners & Sponsors
of The HBCU Experience Movement, LLC

Baker & Baker Realty, LLC

Christopher Baker- CEO/Founder
Instagram: seedougieblake
Facebook: Christopher D. Baker
Email: baker.christopher@gmail.com

Bound By Conscious Concepts

Kathryn Lomax-CEO/Founder
Instagram: msklovibes223
Facebook: Klo-Kathryn Lomax
Contact: (972) 638-9823
Email: Klomax@bbconcepts.com

Dancer NC Dance District

Dr. Kellye Worth Hall
Instagram: divadoc5
Facebook: Kellye Worth Hall
Email: delta906@gmail.com

HBCU Wall Street

Torrence Reed & Jamerus Peyton-CEO/Founders
Facebook: HBCU Wall Street
Email: info@hbcuwallstreet.com

SPGBK

Springbreak Watches (SPGBK)

Kwame Molden- CEO/Founder
Instagram: SPGBK
Facebook: Kwame Molden
Email: info@springbreakwatches.com

Minority Cannabis Business Association

Shanita Penny- President
Instagram- Minority Cannabis
Facebook- MCBA.Org
Twitter- MinCannBusAssoc
LinkedIn- Minority Cannabis Business Association
Email-info@minoritycannabis.org
Website: www.MinorityCannabis.org
Phone: 202-681-2889

The Phoenix Professional Network

DJavon Alston-Owner/Founder
Instagram: thephoenixnetwork757
Facebook: DJavon Alston
Email: thephoenixnetwork757@gmail.com

Never2Fly2Pray

Jeffrey Lee Sawyer: Owner/Founder
Instagram: never2fly2pray
Facebook: Jeffrey Lee
Email htdogwtr@yahoo.com

Allen Financial Solutions

Jay Allen: Owner/Founder
Instagram: jay83allen
Facebook: Jay Allen
Email: allen.jonathan83@gmail.com

Holistic Practitioners

Tianna Bynum: CEO/Founder
Facebook: Tianna Bynum
Email tpb33@georgetown.edu

Journee Enterprises

Fred Whit: CEO/Founder
Facebook: Fred Whit
Instagram: frederickwjr
Email: frederickwjr@yahoo.com

Company: Ashley Little Enterprises, LLC

Ashley Little- CEO/Founder
Facebook: Ashley Little
Instagram: _ashleyalittle
Email: aalittle08@gmail.com

HBCU Pride Nation

CEO/ Founder: Travis Jackson
Instagram: hbcupridenation
Facebook: HBCU Pride Nation
Email: travispjackson@gmail.com

LK Productions

CEO/Founder: Larry King
Instagram: lk_rrproduction
Facebook: Larry King
Email: lk_production@yahoo.com

NXLEVEL TRAVEL (NXLTRVL)

Chief Executive Officer Hercules Conway
Chief Operating Officer Newton Dennis
Instagram-nxlevel
Instagram: herc3k
Facebook-Newton Dennis
Facebook: Hercules Conway
Email Address: info@nxleveltravel.com
Website: NXLEVELTRAVEL.COM

BLKWOMENHUSTLE

CEO/Founder: Lashawn Dreher
Instagram: blkwomenhustle
Facebook: Blk Women Hustle
Email: info@blkwomenhustle.com

PATTERSON, HARDEE & BALLENTINE, P.C.

Certified Public Accountants
Ashlee Brooks
Tax Associate
Email: ashleebrooks@hotmail.com

Campaign
Engineers

Campaign Engineers

Chris Smith, CEO/Founder
Instagram: csmithatl
Email Address: csmith1911@gmail.com

Boardroom Brand LLC

Samuel Brown III, CEO/Founder
Instagram: _gxxdy
Email Address: samuel.brown.three@gmail.com

HBCU 1010

Jahliel Thurman, CEO/Founder
www.hbcu101.com
Instagram: hbcu101
jahlielthurman@gmail.com

Uplift Clothing Apparel

Jermaine Simpson, CEO/Founder
UpliftClothingApparel.com
Instagram: Upliftclothingapparel

AC Events The Luxury Planning Experience

Amy Agbottah, CEO/Founder:
Email Address: amy@amycynthiaevents.com

PIXRUS Photo Booth

Natan Mckenzie, CEO/Founder
Email Address: Natan.mckenzie@gmail.com
Instagram: pixrusghana

MMInvestments

Tarik McAllister, CEO/Founder:
Instagram: MMInvestments
Email Address: tarik@mmibuilders.com

AllThingsLoop

Kenya Nalls, CEO/Founder:
Email Address: staff@allthingsloop.com
Contact Number: 773-939-0680

Historically Black Since

CEO/Founder: Adrena Martin
Instagram: historicallyblacksince
www.hbcusince.com

February First

CEO/Founder: Cedric Livingston
www.februaryfirstmovie.com
Director/Writer February First: A Stride Towards Freedom

HBCU Times

David Staten, Ph.
hbcutimes@gmail.com
Facebook: HBCU Times
Instagram: hbcu_times8892
Bridget Hollis Staten, Ph.D

Swing Into Their Dreams Foundation

Pamela Parker and Lynn Demmons, Co-Founders
Email Address: swingintotheirdreams@gmail.com
Website: swingintotheirdreams.com

Harbor Institute

CEO/Founder: Rasheed Ali Cromwell, JD
Instagram: @theharborinstitute
Facebook: The Harbor Institute
Twitter: @harborinstitute
Email: racromwell@theharborinstitute.com

HBCU Pulse

CEO/Founder Randall Barnes
Website: hbcupulse.com
Instagram: @hbcupulse
Twitter: @thehbcupulse

SwagHer

Vice President Of Sales/Marketing Jarmel Roberson
Website www.swagher.net
instagram: swaghermagazine
Email Address: jroberson@swagher.net

H.E.R. Story Podcast

Janea Jamison|Creator
H.E.R. Story with J. Jamison
#Herstorymovement
IG : @herstory_podcast

HBCU Buzz

LUKE LAWAL JR.
lawal@lcompany.co
Fndr, CEO | (301) 221-1719 @lukelawal
L & COMPANY { *HBCU Buzz | Taper, Inc. | Root Care Health* }

Zoom Technologies, LLC

Torrence Reed - CEO/Founder
Instagram: torrencereed3
Email: support@zoom-technologies.co

KOE

Koereyelle Dubose CEO/Founder
Instagram: koereyelle
Email Address: hi@koereyelle.com

Yard Talk 101

Jahliel Thurman CEO/Founder
Instagram: YardTalk101
Website: YardTalk101.com

Chef Batts

Keith Batts-CEO/Founder
Instagram: chefbatts
Email: booking@chefbatts.com

JOHNSON CAPITAL

Johnson Capital

Marcus Johnson CEO/Founder
Instagram: marcusdiontej
Email: marcus@johnsoncap.com